The Pastor
to Dalits

ISPCK Contextual Theological Education Series No.: 8

The Pastor to Dalits

by
John C.B. Webster

ISPCK
1997

The Pastor to Dalits—Published by the Indian Society for Promoting Christian Knowledge (ISPCK), Post Box 1585, Kashmere Gate, Delhi–110006, under the Indian Contextual Theological Education Series–8

First Edition 1995
Reprinted 1997

Printed at Academy Press, Noida 201301

BY THE SAME AUTHOR

The Study of History and College History Teaching (Editor)

History for College Students (Editor)

History and Contemporary India (Editor)

Popular Religion in the Punjab Today (Editor)

*The Christian Community and Change in
Nineteenth Century North India*

An Introduction to History

The Nirankari Sikhs

The Church and Women in the Third World (Co-Editor)

The Dalit Christians: A History

To
the members of
Crossroads Presbyterian Church
Waterford, Connecticut
1984-1994

who taught me most of what I know
about being a pastor and who at the
same time encouraged me to maintain
my special ties with India and with
the Dalit Christians in particular.

TABLE OF CONTENTS

PREFACE

In September 1992 the Department of Dalit Theology at Gurukul Lutheran Theological College in Madras organized a two day seminar of historians and theologians on my book, *The Dalit Christians: A History*. During that consultation it became apparent not only that the curriculum of the whole practical field in the theological colleges had to be reoriented to address the Dalit reality of Christianity in India, but also that there were few resources available to facilitate such a reorientation. This book was conceived as an attempt to begin filling that gap.

It grew out of conversations a year later with the Rt. Rev. M. Azariah, bishop of the Madras Diocese of the Church of South India. Together we planned a consultation of experienced pastors to both urban and rural Dalits in his diocese. Its purpose was to pool the wisdom already gained from pastoral experience and to generate new knowledge through a joint research project. The consultation was held from August 29 to September 2 and from September 26 to 30, 1994 at the C.S.I. High School for the Deaf in Mylapore, Madras. In November 1994 the Christian Institute of Religious Studies at Baring Union Christian College, Batala, Punjab convened a much smaller, briefer, follow-up consultation of pastors on the same theme.

This book is thus the product of a shared search for understanding among pastors trying to minister to Dalit Christians in two widely separated parts of India. It is an exploratory study undertaken to open up the important subject of ministry to Dalit Christians for reflection and appropriate experimentation throughout the entire Indian Church. At the same time, it is an attempt to gain greater clarity of vision about the pastor's distinctive ministry to Dalits in the midst of their continuing struggle for dignity, equality, and justice. If, in addition to contributing to an increasingly effective ministry to Dalits in India, this book can also serve as a useful resource for those pastoring people living with similar inner and external realities in other societies, that will be an extra benefit. Certainly ministry everywhere can be helped by serious and sympathetic empirical study.

Quite a few people have told me that they find the title of this book misleading, apparently because they consider Dalits and Dalit Christians to be two completely separate and distinct groups of people. I do not. In fact, I think it is precisely the Dalitness in Dalit Christians that most often is not ministered to. In addition, I find many pastors and

Christian Dalits do not draw sharp communal lines between Christian and other Dalits. Thus the title, even if perhaps confusing to some, focuses attention precisely where I think it needs to be focused. While not apologizing for the title, I will apologize for what many might consider a North Indian, and even Punjabi, bias to the historical introduction. As I indicate there, suitable source materials were not easy to find. Many of the best I did find in the All-India publications I consulted happened to come from the North rather than the South.

There are many people I would like to thank for their help in making this book a reality. First and foremost among these is Bishop Azariah who provided ideas, enthusiasm, participants, and all the necessary resources for the Madras consultation. The Rev. Samuel Jacob, Director of the Madras Diocese's Department of Dalit Liberation, and Mr. Anban Thambidorai, Headmaster of the C.S.I. High School for the Deaf, took care of the local arrangements for the consultation. Henry Thiagaraj, Managing Trustee of the Dalit Liberation Education Trust in Madras, put us through two practical experiences which saved the consultation from being totally intellectual. Hilda Rajah of Stella Maris College, V. Devasahayam of Gurukul Lutheran Theological College, and Theophilus Apavoo of Tamilnadu Theological Seminary shared their special expertise with us as guest lecturers. Our Bible study leaders were the Rev. Y.L. Babu Rao and the Rev. Chris Theodore.

Professor Itty Benjamin organized the Batala consultation. Special presentations were given by Dr. Clarence McMullen, Director of the Christian Institute of Religious Studies; the Rev. Dr. James Massey, General Secretary of the I.S.P.C.K. in Delhi; and the Rev. Rashid M. Chaudhary, then Principal-elect and now Principal of Baring Union Christian College. Our Bible study leader was Mr. Nazir Masih, Headmaster of the Milne Memorial School in Dhariwal, Punjab.

I owe a special debt of gratitude to all of the pastors who participated in these consultations for their hard work, for sharing so much of their ministry and of themselves with me, and for the research they carried out for this book. Without them it could not have happened. I am also grateful to all the questionnaire respondents and to all who joined in the group discussions for agreeing to participate in this study. Both they and their pastors have taught me a lot!

The Worldwide Ministries Division of the Presbyterian Church (U.S.A.) and especially its Coordinator for the Middle East and South Asia, the Rev. Dr. Victor Makari, have made my participation in this project, and others like it, possible. I also benefitted greatly from the resources of the libraries of Union Theological Seminary in New York City, Yale Divinity School in New Haven, and Connecticut College in New London. The Rev. Marilyn McNaughten, a fellow Presbyterian minister and a doctoral student in Psychology and Religion at Drew University, read drafts of each chapter and made many helpful suggestions for their improvement. She also served as my conscience when venturing into the field of psychology! The comments and recommendations of the Rev. Carl S. Dudley, Professor of Church & Community and Co-Director of the Center for Social and Religious Research at Hartford Theological Seminary have also proven helpful in preparing the final version of the manuscript. Dr. Joseph Kantaraj was kind enough to translate some Tamil and Mrs. Sandra Louthain put all of the questionnaire data on a computer for me. Finally, my wife, Penny, has once again been a great source of wisdom, encouragement, and practical assistance in writing a book. She did not do all the computer work this time, but she did all the difficult work in making the final manuscript "camera ready" for the publisher.

I dedicate this book to a very special congregation I was privileged to serve as pastor from September 1984 through April 1994.

Waterford, Connecticut   John C. B. Webster
June, 1995

CHAPTER 1

AN HISTORICAL INTRODUCTION

During the final third of the nineteenth century, there were rural Dalit mass conversion movements in several widely separated parts of India. In response to these movements the Protestant missions affected generally placed a teacher/catechist in or near those villages where Dalits were requesting Christian instruction and baptism. If the number of converts was large enough to warrant it, these men remained in the village to become, in effect, pastors, teachers and evangelists to the Dalits there and in the neighboring villages. They acted under the supervision of a district missionary, possibly with an Indian pastor as intermediary, but they were the ones who did the actual pastoring of Dalit converts and congregations.

Today's pastor to Dalits is the heir of those original catechists, teachers, and evangelists, as well as of their successors. From them he/she has inherited a changing legacy of responsibilities, expectations, dilemmas, and insights. This study therefore begins by exploring that legacy from the past. Specifically, it seeks answers to the following questions. Who were these men? What was the pastoral situation they faced? What did pastoring Dalits involve in that situation? How have they, their pastoral situations and work changed over the past century? In what ways are pastors to Dalits today different from their predecessors of earlier generations?

As it has turned out, those questions have not been easy to answer. Despite the fact that this is a history which is national in scope, covers more than one hundred years, and concerns thousands of pastors as well as their congregations, the direct evidence available is very limited indeed. Some promising denominational sources as well as such ecumenical Protestant publications as *Harvest Field*, its successor *National Christian Council Review*, and the *International Review of Missions* were scanned for articles which might supplement materials already in hand in providing answers to the questions mentioned above. Since many denominational sources from southern and western India could not be consulted, this history can be only an exploratory, suggestive, and at times insightful, rather than definitive account. Additional research into those sources may confirm or modify the findings and conclusions given here.

Although the search for relevant evidence proved to be somewhat disappointing, it did reveal four things of great importance to this study. Those people who wrote about Dalits, while often acknowledging the crucial importance of the teacher/catechist to the success of mass movement work, nonetheless were, to judge from their writings, more enamored with "the big picture" concerning Dalits than with either the routine or the trials and tribulations of providing pastoral care for them.[1] Secondly, those who did write about teacher/catechists tended to describe them from an administrative point of view. Their articles and reports present an abstracted, generalized, task-oriented view from above which focuses attention upon issues, problems, and roles instead of upon people. For example, many potentially useful sources discuss only the teacher/catechist's qualifications, training, deployment, support, and required tasks, while ignoring his week-by-week life and work as a pastor to Dalits. Third, in almost every case, these source materials refer to the rural rather than to urban Dalits and their pastors. What happened to Dalit Christians in the towns or cities and how pastors sought to minister to them there is a largely untold story. Finally, the written sources which did prove useful, when taken together, really give the historian two histories at the same time. One is the history of the reality of pastoring Dalits over the past four to six generations; the other is a history of growing awareness of, perceptions of, and insights into that reality. What was the time lag between the inception of the reality itself and the (usually missionary) writer's perception of it, insights into it, and reports about it: one or two years, or one or two generations? Probably that question can be answered only after gathering oral histories from both retired pastors to Dalits and the descendants of earlier generations of pastors to Dalits. However, this preliminary study of written sources must allow the two histories to stand with tensions between them unresolved. In this way it can

---

[1] The report of the Jerusalem (1928) meeting of the International Missionary Council on *The Christian Mission in Relation to Rural Problems* (New York, 1928) and its follow-up report on India by Kenyon L. Butterfield, *The Christian Mission in Rural India* (New York, 1930) took this tendency a step farther. These reports completely ignored the rural (Dalit) congregations and their pastors, probably because their very existence made somewhat problematical the glorious vision of Christian rural reconstruction Butterfield and others had in mind.

serve as a source of questions for further historical investigation just as it has been a source of questions about the pastor to Dalits today.

FROM THE MASS MOVEMENTS TO WORLD WAR I

When the Third Decennial Missionary Conference met in Bombay at the very end of 1892, Dalit mass movements had been going on long enough in several parts of the country for the participants to devote considerable attention to them. While they did not discuss the life and work of the pastor to Dalits, several missionaries did mention the pastoral situation which they and their mass movement workers faced. Perhaps the most direct reference was this comment by the Rev. Samuel Martin, a United Presbyterian missionary in the Punjab.

It is much easier to the convert to gain a theoretical knowledge of Christianity than it is for him to make it his rule of life; to give up the heathen customs that have become a part of his nature almost and adapt his new mode of living to his new belief. It is one of the most perplexing questions we have to solve, how to provide for the proper pastoral supervision of these converts; poor and ignorant and scattered in small groups over a large district; and subjected to annoyance and persecution from their non-Christian neighbours and employers. The spiritual growth and development of the Church depends on the care and instruction of these new converts, and yet the aggressive work must go on.[2]

Later Martin mentioned three life-style changes which he considered essential to bringing the Dalit converts' "mode of life" into greater conformity with their "new belief."

... with regard to the Sabbath -- their dependence on their Hindu and Mahomedan employers makes it hard for them to observe it properly. Their extreme poverty makes it difficult for them to give up the use of carrion, to which some of them have always been accustomed. It is hard for them to adapt themselves to the requirements of the Christian marriage law. It is not strange that a law originally designed for a different race and clime should be hard to adjust to meet the wants of a people who have scarcely ever felt

---

2   S. Martin, "Work among the Depressed Classes and the Masses," *Report of the Third Decennial Missionary Conference held at Bombay, 1892-93* (Bombay, 1893), 22.

the restraints of law in this matter.[3]

As these two excerpts indicate, the aim of pastoral work among Dalits was, for Martin, nothing less than the transformation of individual and social life for a section of the Indian population with many serious vulnerabilities. The other conference participants were in basic agreement. In addition, they made frequent reference to those aspirations for dignity and social advancement which had led Dalits to request Christian instruction and baptism, but which baptism alone, apart from educational and other forms of "uplift work," could not provide. In these discussions it was clear that responsibility for uplift lay with the missions and missionaries rather than with the local teacher/catechists. The other aspect of the pastoral situation mentioned at the conference was that the teacher/catechist was expected to look increasingly to his Dalit congregation rather than to the mission for support. Martin himself considered this essential, even if it meant that these workers would have to be "content with a bare living," because the missions had to employ more workers than they could afford in order to take advantage of the evangelistic opportunities before them.[4]

Some brief descriptions of the teacher/catechist's work in Dalit villages provided by Martin's colleague, Robert Stewart, a few years later give some indication of what it meant to be a pastor to Dalits at the end of the nineteenth century.

He goes from house to house, gets acquainted with the peculiarities of each individual, corrects any wrong impressions which the people may have had respecting Christianity, confirms their opposition to the false religion which they have abandoned, teaches them as fast as he can passages of Scripture, a Bible Catechism, the Ten Commandments, the Lord's Prayer and the fundamental principles of our holy faith, urges them to abandon every form of sin, and exhorts them to commence family and secret prayer. He also meets with them as often as he can -- perhaps every day -- for public worship, and on the Sabbath is expected, not only to conduct a regular religious service and preach, but also to hold a Sabbath School and catechetically instruct all, old and young, in

---

3   *Ibid.*, 23.

4   *Ibid.*, 25.

regard to divine things.[5]
As Stewart pointed out, "His work is emphatically 'precept upon precept, precept upon precept, line upon line, line upon line; here a little and there a little.'"[6]

A fuller and more empathetic picture of the teacher/ catechist emerges in the available sources only at the outbreak of World War I in Godfrey Phillips' book, *The Outcastes' Hope*. Whereas the first pastors to Dalits appear to have been adult converts who had spent a few months or a year at a mission training center receiving special training for the kind of pastoral work described above,[7] Phillips points out that by about 1914 the teacher/catechists were usually Dalits who were children of converts. They had shown promise while receiving an education at their village school and so were sent to a mission boarding school for further training. This teacher/ catechist, in addition to being teacher, preacher, and upholder of Christian discipline as the mission desired, also had to meet the needs and expectations of his Dalit congregation as a local medical practitioner and settler of domestic quarrels.

In oppressions by the caste people, in domestic joys and sorrows, in disputes as to ownership of land or as to village right-of-way, this teacher-catechist is called to be the guide, philosopher and friend of the community which naturally tends to lean hard on any outside help which may be offered.[8]

This the teacher/catechist did amidst great adversity.

He is treated with contempt by the caste people, and badgered for help by the worst sort of the pariahs. At any moment, if he offends the village caste people, they will stop the village barber and washerman from working for him, and sometimes they can cut off his water-supply. He is very poor, for the mission suffers from

---

[5] Robert Stewart, *Life and Work in India* (New edition; Philadelphia, 1899), 262-263.

[6] *Ibid.*, 264.

[7] This is implicit in W. L. Ferguson's discussion of ordination in "The Growth of the Church in the Mission Field: The Telugu Mission of the American Baptist Foreign Mission Society," *International Review of Missions,* I (1912), 692-694. It was probably, of necessity, common practice.

[8] G.E. Phillips, *The Outcastes' Hope or Work Among the Depressed Classes in India* (London, 1915), 68.

chronic deficiency of funds, and while its work is increasing its
grants have decreased, so that the village teachers are perforce kept
at very low rates of pay. Yet he has ambitions for his children, and
sends them away to a town boarding-school, the fees for which are,
by an agreement with the missionary, deducted from his own
salary, making it smaller than ever.

And so Phillips concludes that, "Humanly speaking, he has almost
everything to depress and little enough to encourage him , and it is a
matter of profound thankfulness if he keeps steadily and faithfully at
work in spite of it all."[9]

By the outbreak of World War I the mass movements in many parts
of India had been in existence for over a generation. The pastor to
Dalits was either a convert or the son of convert, with as much as six
years of formal education, who was dealing primarily with converts and
their children.[10] In the C.M.S. Telugu Mission he was responsible
for an average of fifty Christians, whereas in its Punjab Mission he was
responsible for an average of about five hundred.[11] His work was
viewed in almost exclusively religious terms: worship leader, teacher,
and guide in moving towards a new, Christian way of living. The
difficulties he faced were those of anyone trying to introduce religious
and life-style changes into a traditional culture: opposition, persecution,
and a constant struggle to make possible for his children an even better
life than he himself was experiencing. But was there more to it than
that? Perhaps much more was going on than was reported, or perhaps,
as Phillips indicates, the Dalits the teacher/ catechist dealt with were

---

[9] *Ibid.,* 69.

[10] In the Medak area of Andhra Pradesh the Methodists trained
orphan children gathered during the 1897-1900 famine as their original
evangelists whose work was similar to the catechist/teacher among other
missions. Otherwise the early history of the pastor to Dalits there was
similar to that described in this essay. P.Y. Luke and John B. Carman,
Village Christians and Hindu Culture (New York, 1968), 112-115.

[11] These were probably the two extremes. The United Presbyterians, the best in the Punjab at that time, had one catechist/teacher for
about every 175-200 Christians. Henry Madras [Whitehead], "The Mass
Movement Towards Christianity in the Punjab," *International Review of
Missions,* II:3 (1913), 447-448.

simply resigned to their fate as Dalits. [12] Pastoral work at this stage may therefore have been confined largely to moving Dalit inquirers and converts out of such fatalism into a life where grace, hope, and self-discipline could play a greater role.

WORLD WAR I TO INDEPENDENCE

The period between World War I and Independence in 1947 was a much more difficult period for the pastor to Dalits. The old order in which British rule held sway and Christianity enjoyed a certain prestige was being challenged and overthrown. Mahatma Gandhi, other social reformers, and other politicians were now openly competing for the Dalits' allegiance and challenging the Church's effectiveness in dealing with the Dalits' plight. The Depression seriously diminished the economic resources the missions had at their disposal and all mission workers felt the pinch. Yet, in the midst of all this, there was a growing awareness in Christian circles that the mass movements had made the Indian Church a rural Church and the well-being of rural Christian communities therefore became a major missionary concern. One of the signs of this concern was an increase in serious studies and analyses of the rural church. None of these made the pastor to Dalits its centerpiece, but his life and work now came into sharper focus than before.

A survey conducted in 1917 indicated that many missions throughout India were now training two levels of rural workers. [13] At the lower level were rural Dalit adults with at most a primary education. These men, along with their wives, were being trained, either for three years or for three months supplemented by summer refresher courses, to return to the villages as teacher/ catechists. The higher course was taught to rural Dalit youth who had studied at mission boarding schools through the sixth or eighth standard. These students would then

---

[12] *Ibid.*, 16.

[13] T. Law, "The Training of Village Workers," in H. D. Griswold, ed., *Village Evangelization (No. 2) Being Papers Read at the 17th Annual Meeting of the North India Conference of Christian Workers, held in Mussoorie, June 19-22, 1917* (Mysore, 1917), 5-29. Law, a C.M.S. missionary in Aligarh, U.P., included reports from missionaries of several different denominations in North India engaged in training village workers; all of the reports he received from the South were sent by Anglicans.

complete a fuller theological course and become ordained rural pastors with supervisory responsibilities for the catechists in their areas.

In the Punjab, this led to the "circuit system," a new pattern of ministry to rural Dalits started by the United Presbyterians, the pioneer mass movement mission there, and adopted by the other Punjab missions. Instead of having a large number of teacher/catechists residing in a large number of villages, the missions now moved to having a smaller number of better educated pastors, each responsible for a wider "territory" of more villages than the teacher/catechist had been serving. These pastors were to train and work with such resident volunteer lay leadership as lambardars, chaudhries, and church panchayat members within each village.[14] The paid catechists were then gradually phased out.

In the South, however, the catechist seems to have remained a fixture in the rural ministry. His life is described in a composite portrait of a Telugu teacher/evangelist published in 1918. As a boy he attended his village school. After completing three standards there, he went to the Mission Boarding School through the seventh standard and then had two years of teacher training. Now, at the age of 22, he is posted in a village where he is in charge of the school, pastor to the village congregation, and evangelist to his own and neighboring villages. During week day mornings and afternoons he teaches, with little equipment, between one and four classes of inattentive and irregular students simultaneously; at night he instructs adult inquirers and catechumens. On Sundays he leads morning and evening worship, holds special adult classes, and visits the sick. However, there is more to his work than that!

Being the only man of any education in his hamlet, he is general clerk for the people, and so helps them in writing and reading letters. He checks their accounts with the merchant of the village, and draws up agreements or promissory notes. He is often called upon to arbitrate some quarrel, perhaps over a lost cow or some

---

[14] This process of change among United Presbyterians may be seen in Frederick and Margaret Stock, *People Movements in the Punjab with special reference to the United Presbyterian Church* (Pasadena, 1975), 141-152. One can see it at work also in the description of the Kasur station of the Punjab Mission of the Presbyterian Church in the U.S.A. in *Survey of the Evangelistic Work of the Punjab Mission of the Presbyterian Church in the U.S.A.* (N.P., 1929), 205-207.

trivial matter, or it may be a more serious affair such as a lost wife. In every kind of trouble his advice is sought. He may perhaps dispense a little medicine, such as quinine, etc. When he visits Ellore he often makes purchases for his people, and carries a letter or two for the post. At festival seasons he improvises decorations from leaves and paper with great ingenuity and some artistic ability. He also has to arrange and look after the small mission property, and help in its repairs, and raise at least half the cost of the same among his people, in addition to receiving the collections for various objects.[15]

Here is a portrait of the teacher/catechist as servant, not just of the mission but of his Dalit congregation as well. Another article on the Telugu teacher/catechist published twelve years later in 1930 adds another telling dimension to this side of the catechist's life and work.

A large amount of the teacher's time is taken up with trying to help the Christians in their troubles with the caste people and their squabbles among themselves. He is always expected to be the champion of his little flock and often incurs great personal inconvenience and sometimes danger on their account. I have known teachers more than once go to prison because they stood up for their villagers in a case of injustice. True indeed it is that they must espouse the cause of the oppressed, or lose their influence with the people, and this takes hours and hours of their time. It often involves long and frequently fruitless journeys to the court in a distant village to attend cases on behalf of their village flocks.[16]

A composite picture of the teacher/catechist in Travancore also indicates that he spent a lot of time dealing with his Dalit parishioners' complaints and grievances against their neighbors, most often over encroachment, property damage by cattle, and assault. [17] The Wisers in

---

[15] E.S. Tanner, "The Telugu Teacher-Evangelist," *C.M.S. Mass Movement Quarterly* (January 1918), 14. (Hereafter this will be referred to as *MMQ*.)

[16] Ernest Evitt, "The Telugu Mission Agent," *MMQ* (September 1930), 35-36. See also C.W. Posnett, "Among Baptized Outcastes," *International Review of Missions,* XV (April 1926), 237.

[17] W.S. Hunt, "A Travancore Worker and His Work," *MMQ* (September 1930), 44.

their classic anthropological study of the Indian village, *Behind Mud Walls*, reported the same thing among Dalit Christians in Karimpur, U.P. The Dalit Christians there clearly expected the missionary to serve as their patron in all of their litigations, something which the Wisers refused to do.[18]

However, this aspect of the pastoral situation of the rural pastor to Dalits appears to have received its fullest and most thoughtful treatment in the Punjab. Judging from the printed reports, quarrels and litigation were so common among the Punjabi Dalit Christians as to have been integral to their way of life. Marriages and bride price were the most frequently mentioned causes of quarrels among the Dalit Christians themselves, but fights with their pastors were referred to as well. Disgruntled Dalit Christians (sometimes led by disgruntled catechists) moved back and forth between the older, established missions and the newer ones who were not party to comity agreements, such as the Salvation Army, Seventh Day Adventists, Roman Catholics, and independent Indian missions. A Board of Economic Inquiry of the Punjab found that rural Dalit Christians were more often mistreated by zamindars than were other village menials. Among the reasons given were that the zamindars resented their conversion, their independence, their children's education, as well as their "uncalled for insolence which annoys and angers the Zamindars."[19]

Two not incompatible types of explanations were offered for all of this contention, strife, and "uncalled for insolence." One was socio-logical and the other was psychological. The Rev. Barakat Ullah attributed it to the missionary image of the Dalit Christians as "ignorant honest souls" and especially to the mission "help system" developed to protect these "ignorant honest souls" from their oppressors.

The missionaries were the *mai bap* of their people, helping them in all matters, whenever and wherever their help was required. If a money-lender threatened Christians, they went to the missionary who was ready to help the poor against the rich; if a *zamindar* gave less to his Christian hands than was their due, the missionary's

---

18 Charlotte Viall Wiser and William H. Wiser, *Behind Mud Walls* (New York, 1930), 63-64.

19 R.B. Nesbitt, "Disabilities of Village Christians," *National Christian Council Review* (June 1926), 328-329.

help was requisitioned; if the police maltreated Christian villagers, the missionary used his influence and the police were taught the lesson of letting Christians alone. . . . If petty Government officials wanted *begar* (forced labour) from village Christians, the missionary prohibited them from working and reported such cases to high officials. In short, the missionary made it his business, as far as lay in his power, to see that no harm, no oppression, no tyranny, no injustice of any kind, should come near his Christians.[20]

This "help system," while noble in its intentions and in some of its results, was being misused by Dalit Christians.

They saw that whenever they reported their numerous cases of injustice and maltreatment to the missionary, the proudest quailed before his eyes and "ate dust" before him. This they witnessed for over half a century, with the result that the pendulum has swung to the other side. The tables have turned, and those that were once oppressed and downtrodden are now, trusting to the missionary's influence, often insolent, rude and overbearing. They will now not only not put up with injustice, but will often be 'cheeky' to their lawful masters and endeavour to escape the just punishment of their misdeeds. The name of the missionary and the *babu* (the local preacher) are still powerful weapons which they unscrupulously use to bring about their own selfish ends.[21]

To use the Wiser's terminology, Dalit Christians played off the mission as their new patron against their old patron, the landlord. The presence and influence of this new patron gave them a new-found and almost intoxicating power in the struggle for status and gain within the village. If the mission was unwilling or unable to perform satisfactorily in the role of patron, Dalit Christians would often either seek other mission patrons to replace it or simply refuse financial support for the local teacher/catechist. However, this 'help system" was breaking down under the impact of nationalism. It had been based upon missionary cultivation of friendships with well-placed government officials, but now the government was becoming more Indianized and missionary influence was decreasing.

---

[20] Barakat Ullah, "An Aspect of the Mass Movement Problem in the Punjab," *National Christian Council Review* (May 1927), 292-293.

[21] *Ibid.,* 294-295

J. C. Heinrich, while earlier attributing the conflict among rural Dalit Christians to overcrowded living conditions and the frustration of educated but unemployed Christian young people,[22] later turned to a psychological explanation. His book, *The Psychology of a Suppressed People*, was based upon an analysis of current psychological theory, of studies of Black Americans, and of his own experience with Dalit Christians in the Punjab. Its basic premise was that

> the craving for self-expression and superiority is such a basic biological urge, a major craving, as necessary in the struggle for existence as is the sex urge and the urge for self-preservation. When blocked its natural result is a manifestation of the emotion of rage and anger. Open expression of these emotional reactions are usually inexpedient and bring results inimical to personal welfare.[23]

However, emerging groups of suppressed people, like the Dalit converts to Christianity, do express their rage and anger either directly or indirectly. As an example of direct expression of this pent-up rage and anger, Heinrich cited the report of one district missionary that "the police records in his district show an increase in major crimes, including murder, among the depressed classes since they have embraced Christianity."[24] However, the expression of this anger was more apt to be indirect, generally through "establishing a pseudo-superiority by lowering and disparaging rivals or apparent superiors."[25] Both conversion and the "help system" together, it would seem, had reduced Dalit inhibitions about expressing their suppressed inner rage to the point where they were constantly quarrelling either with their oppressors or with each other.

Heinrich went on to devote an entire chapter to the impact which the Dalit Christians' new-found ability to express anger had upon the pastor and teacher/catechist. One district conference of such workers reported that

> they all had to fight for their lives, especially at the beginning of

---

[22]   J.C. Heinrich, "Blessed are the Peacemakers." *United Church Review* (September 1934), 228-229.

[23]   (London, 1937), 52.

[24]   *Ibid.*, 57.

[25]   *Ibid.*, 60.

their ministry, to keep from getting under the thumbs of their people. Efforts were constantly made to entangle them in shady transactions or to find some way to humiliate them. The exaggerated craving for superiority that resulted in the oppression, the minimizing, and the undervaluing of others was so common among their people that its encounter was a well-defined part of the experience of every one of the workers.[26]

This was especially apparent when the pastor or teacher/ catechist had to collect the money necessary to develop or maintain a self-supporting local church. His arrival would be greeted with such taunts as, "Well, have you come around to take the very skin off our backs?" or " Do you never think of anything but your belly?" or "the old ass comes braying every other day, the old ass comes braying every other day."[27] Given the fact that both the pastor and the teacher/catechist also had to make their own adjustments to the demands of their missionary supervisors and deal with their own feelings of inferiority in relation to the missionaries, such treatment from those they came to the village to help was particularly hard to deal with. Indeed, pastors found the "feeling of profound and subtle antipathy" toward their people difficult to avoid.[28]

Heinrich's insights into Dalit anger were both extremely important and very controversial at the time. Unfortunately, it is not clear from his study how long it took Dalits to "emerge" from suppression to the point where they could express their pent-up rage, either directly or indirectly. Barakat Ullah indicated that "uncalled for insolence" was as old as the mass movements themselves and not an exclusively second or third generation phenomenon. Heinrich also did not explain how pastors to Dalits dealt theologically or pastorally with Dalit anger, especially when it was directed at the pastor himself. He did indicate that the Dalit Christians' enormous emotional energy, if directed towards solid achievement, could make a great positive difference in the life of the Church,[29] but he did not show how the pastors were doing this.

---

26 *Ibid.*, 38-39.

27 *Ibid.,* 39-40.

28 *Ibid.,* 73.

29 *Ibid.,* 144.

This points to another problem which the rural pastor to Dalits had to face, at least in North India. The Tambaram conference of the International Missionary Council in 1938 brought together a number of studies of the rural Dalit church in its report, *The Economic Basis of the Church*. These showed that the stewardship of rural Dalit Christians was not simply the result of group psychology; it was also a consequence of the huge financial drain caused by that network of biradari obligations in which rural Dalit Christians were invariably enmeshed. These obligations included paying annual membership fees as well as one's family's share in the costs of marriages (the biggest expense), community feasts, other special levies, and even gifts to non-Christian religious functionaries. These mandatory contributions left all Dalits, Christians included, in perpetual debt. Christians who did not contribute lost respect and standing in the biradari which not only provided spouses for their children but also served as their sole source of security and community within village society. Many rural pastors tried to create Christian biradaris in order to keep what was good but eliminate what they found unChristian and unnecessarily expensive in the traditional system. However, these could be established only in villages where the number of Christians was large enough to maintain an independent biradari of their own.

Two other noteworthy developments round out this picture of the pastor to Dalits between World War I and Independence. One was the growing disparity between the pastor's life-style and that of his village congregations. Pastors, and increasingly teacher/catechists were now products of the mission boarding school; their values and priorities were being shaped as much by the town and the missionary as by the village, especially in the areas of health, hygiene and education.[30] The Wisers told the story of the pastor in Karimpur who, when his brother died, faced enormous pressure from relatives to claim his ancestral rights as a Bhangi in another village. What made him decide against opting for the security (and degradation) which serving as a Bhangi provided was his wife's plea not to return his daughters to that way of life. In Karimpur itself the pastor faced further pressure, and even a school boycott, when he sought to get his son educated in the local school.[31]

The other development was what might be termed a crisis in the

---

[30] Ernest Evitt, "The Telugu Mission Agent," 35.

[31] *Behind Mud Walls*, 66-76.

Punjabi "circuit system" described earlier. In an effort to make their rural congregations more self-supporting, the missions had expanded the territories of their pastors to include more and more villages to share the necessary financial burden. However, the size of their parishes had clearly reached the point where meaningful pastoral care for Dalits was becoming almost impossible. In a survey authorized by the Punjab Synod of the United Church of Northern India in late 1945, S.N. Talibuddin reported that

(a) The parish of each Pastor contains 20 to 60 villages scattered over an area of 10 to 20 square miles. (b) The means of transportation at the disposal of Pastor is the bicycle, in addition to the occasional use of bus and train services. During certain parts of the year the bicycle is not very useful because of poor roads. (c) It is not possible for the Pastor to visit the different groups in his parish more than 1 to 4 times during the year. (d) Sunday Services can be held only in one fifth of the area of each parish. (e) Communion Services are held about 4 times a year in places where Pastors reside, in other places not,more frequently than once a year.[32]

Given these logistics, the pastors simply could not provide the kind of basic care which the village teacher/catechist had given earlier: frequent worship, scriptural teaching, visiting the sick, settling disputes, and the like. "The three items of his ministry that are affected most by insufficient visitation are, services of worship, preparation of candidates for church membership and church finances."[33] This problem was probably not unique to the Punjab or even to the "circuit system," but existed wherever the Depression's impact upon mission budgets had forced the pace of self-support in rural Dalit congregations.

As Independence approached, the pastor to Dalits was still a rural Dalit but he had become better educated, with up to ten years of formal education. In some cases he was now an ordained pastor rather than a catechist/teacher. Moreover, he was dealing not just with converts but with second and even third generation Christians as well. The range of his activities seems to have broadened considerably in the secular realm and the competition he faced for Dalit loyalty from other Christian and

---

[32] S.N. Talibuddin, "A Study of Self-Supporting Churches in the Punjab," *The United Church Review* (July 1947), 325.

[33] *Ibid.*, 326.

non-Christian groups was intensifying. In addition, there was the anger among a newly liberated people to cope with, especially when it was directed at the pastor himself. Perhaps such anger was not new during this period, but only newly understood because more fully and frequently expressed. However, it does lead one to wonder whether in this period the pastor to Dalits was still leading his people as before or whether they were in fact now leading him, especially in those areas where pastoral care was, almost of necessity, becoming more perfunctory. It was a difficult time for pastors to Dalits.

SINCE INDEPENDENCE

Independence in 1947 radically altered the context in which the pastor to Dalits lived and worked. The rulers of independent India introduced a secular democracy with an adult franchise which made even Dalits eligible to vote; expanded educational opportunities greatly, even in the villages; encouraged industrialization which increased the rate of migration from the villages to the towns and cities; and implemented a policy of compensatory discrimination to help Dalits and other disadvantaged groups enjoy their rightful share of the benefits of democracy and development. In the churches the Dalit mass movements came to an end and so too did the missionary "help system." Power was transferred from foreign missionary to Indian hands and the churches underwent considerable internal reorganization as church unions occurred. The urban Christian elites tended to dominate the new ecclesiastical structures and their priorities became the mission and ministry priorities of the Indian churches; Dalits and their pastors were largely ignored. However, beginning in the 1970s, Dalit Christians began to come into their own as a distinct entity both within the churches and within Indian society as a whole. It is not possible to trace all the developments which have affected the pastoral situation and ministry of the pastor to Dalits since Independence. Instead the more significant findings of several empirical studies will be highlighted.

The first of these studies, the chapter on "Rural Church Leadership" in E.Y. Campbell's *The Church in the Punjab,* is the fullest and finest portrait of the pastor to Dalits available in the scholarly literature so far. In it can be seen both continuities with and changes from the past. The village pastor was still a villager who received his primary education in his village, but he has now completed his secondary education in or near a city, where urban life and its values have taken hold of him. Following matriculation he attended a theological seminary to receive professional training as a "spiritual father, teacher and guide,"[34] after which he was ordained and assigned to a village congregation. There the people spoke a different language from that of the classroom and besieged him with requests and situations for which theological seminary had not prepared him. The pastor to Dalits, now much better educated than his predecessors, has become caught between the greater expectations of the larger church and of his profession, on the one hand, and of his rural Dalit congregation, on the other.

If the preacher seeks to maintain professional and educational standards he runs the danger of losing the interest and confidence of his people. If he centers his efforts on the needs and abilities of his village Christians he finds his qualifications for urban life and ministry losing ground. A pastor known for his identification with village life and thought is branded as "rural". His legitimate aspirations regarding the higher education of his children in a middle class urban environment are frustrated by low income and the lack of influence and acquaintance in higher professional circles. Some few men, of exceptional ability, training, or motivation succeed in growing both intellectually and in the practical skills of the rural ministry -- but they are the exceptions.[35]

At the heart of the pastor's dilemma, as described by Campbell, is the secular-sacred conflict posed in the frequently asked question, "Is it the padre's job to be the leader in the temporal affairs of the congregation or only the spiritual?".[36] Temporal affairs continue to take up a lot of the pastor's time, just as before Independence. Moreover, Campbell noted that the spiritual was becoming increasingly marginalized as more and more rural Christians were looking to the politicians and the political parties for temporal leadership; the pastors saw the men either drifting away from the church into politics or bringing political concerns for "security, social and economic mobility, education, and full rights

---

[34] E.Y. Campbell, *The Church in the Punjab: Some Aspects of its Life and Growth* (Lucknow, 1961), 50.

[35] *Ibid.*

[36] *Ibid.*, 52.

before the law" into church meetings.[37] The sacred-secular conflict also
affected the Dalit Christians' sense of their own identity. Were they
"backward" (a secular category) and thus entitled to as many backward
class benefits as they could get, or were they "Christians" (a religious
category) who belonged to a progressive community and so denied
themselves such benefits?[38]

This sacred-secular dilemma was by no means confined to rural
pastors in the Punjab. Alter and Jai Singh found urban pastors in Delhi
had both the same sacred professional role as their rural counterparts
(i.e., leading Sunday worship, officiating at such special functions as
baptisms and marriages, visiting parishioners at home several times a
year) and a secular role which involved them in helping parishioners
find jobs, providing assistance for them during periods of
unemployment, enabling them to get their children enrolled in schools,
and intervening with the police when they get into trouble.[39] Urban
and rural pastors have played leading roles in the Dalit Christians'
political struggle against religious discrimination in the award of
Scheduled Caste benefits, a struggle which affects their sense of identity
in the manner Campbell described.[40] In fact, this sacred-secular
dilemma can also be seen in the ways in which the Christian gospel
itself has been understood and celebrated among Dalit Christians. For
example, Maqbul Caleb found Sunday worship services in a Punjabi
village to be so exclusively "sacred" as to make no connection at all to
the secular realities of the Dalit congregation's lives. In "coming to
Jesus" through both the singing and the preaching, the congregation

---

[37] *Ibid.*, 53.

[38] This issue seems to have been a class issue among Christians.
Rural Dalit Christians in their poverty wanted to avail themselves of every
benefit they could get; in their mind there was no conflict between their
Christian and Dalit identities. Urban, generally better-off Christians did not
want "backwardness" tarnishing the Christian community's progressive
image. *Ibid.*, 55-56.

[39] James P. Alter and Herbert Jai Singh, *The Church in Delhi*
(Lucknow, 1961), 84-85, 102. These are inferences drawn from references
both to the pastor's role in general and to the (usually Chamar) *basti*
Christians.

[40] John C.B. Webster, *The Dalit Christians: A History* (Second
edition; Delhi, 1994), 187-196, 235-236.

was drawn temporarily out of their village world to such an extent that afterwards they could see no meaning in their worship for their everyday life.[41] Lionel Caplan in his study of "CSI Western Church" in Madras, a congregation that had been about fifty percent Dalit, found, not a total separation of the sacred and secular as in that Punjabi village, but a marked preference for a sacred as opposed to a secular understanding both of the sources of adversity and affliction (serious issues for Dalits, as one might expect) and of how these are to be dealt with. Since the missionaries and elite churches have dismissed popular understandings of misfortune which locate these in the realm of the sacred (e.g., evil spirits, divine punishment, etc.), many lower class Christians had turned to fundamentalists and Pentecostals, whose views were much closer to their own and whose ways of healing made better religious sense to them.[42] Recently, liberation theologians and preachers have tried to integrate the sacred and secular into a wholistic view of the Dalit Christian and general Dalit struggle for dignity, equality, and justice. They have called for "a spirituality of combat,"[43] but have left unclear how such a spirituality is to be nurtured.

Campbell describes three rural pastors who exemplify three creative ways of relating the sacred and the secular in pastoring Dalits. The first pastor concentrates upon the spiritual. His home and church are a spiritual center to which people come for daily morning and evening worship. He is simple, direct and sincere in talking with his own people and with others. He is concerned about their temporal affairs but will not take up questionable cases. The second is a very friendly and sociable man whose home is a center of community hospitality where people gather day and night. He trains and shares leadership with lay leaders from the village congregations under his care, which he can visit only monthly. Worship under his leadership is enthusiastic and the

---

[41] Maqbul Caleb, "Christian Sunday Worship in a Punjabi Village," in John C.B. Webster, ed., *Popular Religion in the Punjab Today* (Delhi, 1974), 113-118. Most of the sermons for village (Dalit) worship in Andhra Pradesh summarized by Luke and Carman also fail to connect the gospel message to the secular realities of Dalit life in the village. *Op. cit.*, 139-143.

[42] *Ibid.*, 224-240.

[43] John C.B. Webster, *The Dalit Christians: A History*, 192 & 237.

singing excellent. The third pastor is a political as well as a
community leader. His home is a mini-darbar to which his people
come as much in groups as individually. He is their acknowledged
champion and they in turn are very loyal to him and to the Church. [44]
All three, regardless of style, appear to be generally unrepresented and
silent in the councils of the wider church; their dominant role is with
their own people and with those who affect their people's lives in the
villages.

Neither Campbell nor other scholars have dealt directly with the
problem of Dalit rage and anger during this period. They do provide
ample evidence that such anger, whether directed at other Dalit
Christians, at the Government for its religious discrimination, or at
Church authorities for caste discrimination is a continuing fact of life.
Alter and Jai Singh found that in Delhi pastors seemed to contend with
more "party politics" in Dalit than in more middle class or English
language congregations.[45] Caplan's report from Madras was somewhat
different.

> The clergymen with whom I discussed this matter almost
> invariably mentioned and took delight in the deference shown the
> minister by members of lower-class churches. They respect his
> intellect, his learning, and vocation. His opinions are assiduously
> sought, and his participation in the lives of parishioners sincerely
> canvassed and genuinely appreciated. . . . And though several saw
> congregational politics as a difficult problem to cope with, most
> thought it rarely got out of hand, although everyone knows of
> instances where it obviously did.[46]

In July 1983 a small group of recent United Theological College
graduates in Bangalore, after three days' reflection on their pastoral
experience among Dalits since graduation, lifted up as their most
important priority in ministry to Dalits, "to remove all feelings of
inferiority among them and to instill within them a sense of personal

---

[44] *Op. cit.*, 57-61.

[45] *Ibid.*, 112.

[46] Lionel Caplan, *Class and Culture in Urban India: Fundamentalism in a Christian Community* (Oxford, 1987), 111-112. This stood in
contrast to the treatment (often Dalit) pastors received in elite
congregations which accepted them as pastors performing their pastoral
duties, but did not welcome them socially.

dignity, of self-respect, and of responsibility."[47] This would seem to reinforce Caplan's view.

Finally, the logistical problem of providing adequate pastoral care, both to widely dispersed rural congregations and to new migrants as yet unattached to any urban congregation,[48] has continued on in the post-Independence period. In the Punjab, where the office of paid catechist seems largely to have vanished, some pastors like those Campbell described have found helpful ways of keeping in meaningful contact with their congregations; others, Campbell says, have been overwhelmed by the enormity of the challenge and so do little.[49] In the Medak area of Andhra Pradesh the catechist system was still in place in the 1960s. There, within the Church of South India, the actual pastoring of Dalits was done by the unordained resident evangelist, while ordained pastors played an administrative and supervisory role, making only infrequent visits to administer the sacraments. Moreover, evangelists paid far more attention to the congregations in the villages where they themselves lived than to those in the "second villages" for which they were also responsible.[50] The result has been a growing problem of perfunctory pastoral care and inadequate Christian nurture for rural Dalit congregations. Andrew Wingate, in studying the conversion to Islam in 1981 of Dalit Christians in two villages near Meenakshipuram, attributed those conversions in no small part to pastoral neglect and inadequate pastoral care.[51] Given the ever-present temptation and occasional pressures to revert to Hinduism so as to qualify for Scheduled Caste benefits Dalit Christians having been facing since 1950, the logistics of care and nurture remain, as the United Theological College group testified, major pastoral concerns.

It is almost impossible to generalize with confidence about either the pastor to Dalits or his/her pastoral situation, as both have become more

---

[47] Christianity and the Scheduled Castes: Ministry and Mission (Unpublished).

[48] James P. Alter and Herbert Jai Singh, *op. cit.*, 113 & 143.

[49] *Op. cit.*, 57.

[50] P.Y. Luke and John B. Carman, *op. cit.*, 112-126.

[51] Andrew Wingate, "A Study of Conversion from Christianity to Islam in Two Tamil Villages," *Religion and Society*, XXVIII (December 1981), 8 & 20.

diversified over the half century since Independence. Given this complexity and the paucity of relevant source materials, only two concluding generalizations about this period may be offered here. The first is that the pastor to Dalits now appears to be even better educated than his predecessors were. Most now hold a B.Th., B.D., or equivalent theological degree. While education has enhanced their potential effectiveness, it has also tended to remove them both geographically and culturally, especially from most of their rural congregations. The second is that being a pastor to Dalits has become an increasingly demanding and difficult responsibility. Dalit Christians are changing psychologically, economically, politically, socially and culturally as the world around them also changes. The churches are beginning to take notice, but really do not know what to do or what kind of direction to offer. Pastors to Dalits either have found their own particular niche, or are "working out their calling with fear and trembling," or else have given up and become simply Christian pujaris.

THE PRESENT STUDY

This brief historical survey has provided a suggestive starting point for the empirical study which follows. Specifically, it has indicated what the potentially significant areas for investigation might be, what kinds of questions should be asked, and what the most appropriate components of the study's "setting" might therefore be. Therefore, the chapters which follow are based upon this particular reading of history rather than upon a particular body of relevant theory. Like the history, the empirical study is exploratory rather than rigorously scientific in nature. The manner in which the research was carried out is set forth here so that the value of the conclusions arrived at may be properly assessed.

The research procedure was developed with a two stage consultation of experienced pastors to Dalits in mind. The first stage was devoted to gathering the accumulated wisdom taught by pastoral experience. Each of the nineteen participating pastors brought a completed parish information form (Appendix B) as well as three recent sermons in English translation to the opening session. Four gave presentations on being a pastor to rural Dalits, to urban working class Dalits, to urban middle class Dalits, and to Dalit Christian women respectively. These and some more generalized presentations, as well as the discussion which all the presentations provoked, provided the "received wisdom" on the subject which was to be tested by getting input from Dalit parishioners. For that purpose, we then developed a questionnaire/ interview schedule for a sample of Dalit members of their congregations (Appendix E). The pastors translated this questionnaire into Tamil so that all respondents would be asked the same questions in the same words.

During the three week interval between the first and second session of the consultation, each pastor administered the questionnaire to ten Dalit members of the same parish within his/her pastorate described in the parish information form. In most cases the questionnaire was used as an interview schedule; in some it was simply filled out by the respondent. In addition, the author interviewed each pastor individually and also met with a group of Dalits for discussion in 17 of the 19 parishes. The interview schedules used for the personal interview and group discussion are given in Appendices C and D.

The second session of the consultation was devoted primarily to the questionnaire data. This included collating answers to key questions as well as developing categories for classifying the answers to open-ended questions. Time permitted sharing preliminary totals on about half of the questions and making only a few correlations, comparing answers of rural and urban, male and female, poor, middle class and "in between" respondents. These quick calculations provided the basis for discussions of pastoral priorities in the areas of worship, preaching, Christian education, pastoral care and visitation, social service and social action, local church government, the pastor's personal life, and the diocese. With those discussions the consultation ended.

Since that consultation was held in Madras, these pastors are referred to in the pages which follow as "the Madras pastors." Another much smaller and shorter consultation was later held in Batala, Punjab. Thus reference is made to "the Batala pastors" as well. In Batala the pastors also filled in parish information forms and discussed presentations on ministry to rural and urban Dalits as well as to Dalit Christian women. They also shared their perceptions of how their Dalit parishioners would have answered those questions in the Madras questionnaire for which preliminary results were available as well as their own views of pastoral priorities in the areas of ministry mentioned above. This input from the Batala pastors is used here primarily as a check against regional bias. It is expected that there are some things which all Dalit Christians have in common and other things which they do not because either their regional or their denominational circumstances vary; these variations can cause differences just as variations in rural or urban location, sex, education, and class do. The Batala pastors provide help in determining both the points at which it is safe to generalize from the Madras study to all of India and the points at which it is not safe to.

The parish information forms, presentations`and discussions, as well as the personal interviews with pastors, provide the data on which chapter three is based. Chapter four is an analysis of the pastors' sermons. Chapter five is based primarily upon the responses to the questionnaire. These are supplemented by the author's notes on group discussions with Dalit parishioners. Chapter six seeks to integrate the discussions of pastoral priorities with the material presented in the previous chapters. Finally, chapter two is based on a reading of scholarly literature about Dalits in general. Some of this literature helped give shape to the parish information form and questionnaire; some was consulted only after that data had been collected. Since the study focuses primarily on perceptions, the material in chapter two is used both to "explain" and to challenge the perceptions presented in chapters three and five.

As this discussion of research method indicates, the study which follows is exploratory and deliberately provocative. Like the foregoing history, it seeks to be national in scope but in fact draws most of its material from only one part of the country. It seeks to hold up a mirror in which pastors to Dalits might see themselves and their ministries. Perhaps even its obvious flaws, as well as its strengths, can serve to stimulate reflection, discussion, and further inquiry from which pastors, Dalit Christians, and the whole Church in India can benefit.

CHAPTER 2

THE SETTING

Setting has many dimensions and aspects. The historical survey in the preceding chapter indicated what some of the more crucial ones for pastoral ministry to Dalits might be. This chapter draws upon the work of social scientists in order to describe those more fully in their present context. It assumes that the setting of pastoral ministry to Dalit Christians today is first and foremost a Dalit setting. Christian Dalits are Dalits; they either live in or come from a Dalit world. An understanding of the Dalit world thus provides the most fruitful perspective from which to understand the Christians within it or emerging from it. Moreover, the body of scholarly research on Dalits in general is so much better than the research on Christian Dalits in particular that this choice becomes a virtual necessity. Since the Dalit world is not a uniform world throughout India, samples from different parts of the country are included to indicate where the points of similarity and difference might lie. This procedure should enhance the value of the entire study beyond the small area of South India from which its most detailed data was gathered. The chapter begins by examining the Dalits' rural and urban social settings because these really shape the Dalit world and exercise the greatest influence upon Dalit lives. It then reviews the available literature on Dalit psychology to see how those settings have affected Dalits psychologically. Finally, it describes the particular ecclesiastical setting from which the main body of data is drawn.

THE RURAL SETTING

The jati has been the basic social unit in the Indian village. Members of the same jati lived together in the same section of the village and most of their social relationships have been with each other. Each jati has a traditional occupation, even if all of its members have not actually gained any or all of their livelihood from it. The jatis have been ranked in a hierarchy of social precedence according to the degree of ritual purity or pollution associated with their traditional occupations. The ownership and control of the land has also been an important determinant of status within the village because the entire village economy is dependent upon agriculture. On both counts Dalits rank at the very bottom of the village hierarchy. Their traditional occupations (sweeping, leather work, etc.) have been considered so polluting as to make them untouchable. Those not engaged in their jati's traditional occupation have generally served as menial servants in the village; very few have owned land outright and only a small percentage have enjoyed tenancy rights.

Perhaps the best way to understand how this caste system actually functions in the village is through an examination of what William Wiser called the Hindu jajmani system.[1] Wiser saw the village as a interconnected whole held together by a network of patron-client relationships between members of each jati and members of the other jatis. Thus, for example, each carpenter in the village had his own clientele or jajmani established through custom and passed on from generation to generation.

The relationship fixes responsibilities both on the carpenter and the one whom he serves. The carpenter during the sowing season must remove and sharpen the plough point once or twice a week. During the harvest he must keep sickles sharp and renew handles as often as demanded. He must be ready to repair a cart whenever called upon by a customer, or to make minor repairs on the customer's house. In exchange he receives at each harvest, twenty-eight pounds of grain, for every plough owned by his client.[2]

The services which other jatis had to offer their patrons differed according to their occupations, but members of all the jatis in the village were interrelated in a service capacity. "Each serves the others. Each in turn is master. Each in turn is servant."[3] Moreover, such reciprocal relationships were not confined to the economic domain, but included the ceremonial life of the village as well.

As the example of the carpenter illustrates, clients received payments

---

[1] William Henricks Wiser, *The Hindu Jajmani System: A Socio-Economic System Interrelating Members of a Hindu Village Community in Services* (Lucknow, 1936). Wiser based this study upon data gathered between 1925 and 1930 in Karimpur, U.P., the same village described in *Behind Mud Walls*.

[2] *Ibid.*, 5-6.

[3] *Ibid.*, 10.

in cash or kind for the regular services rendered to their patrons. Such payments were rooted in custom and were not the same for all. In addition, clients also received extra payments for customary services rendered on such occasions as births, weddings, funerals and special pujas in their patrons' families. The other type of compensation clients received from their patrons were a number of vital concessions or perquisites. These also varied according to custom, but included such things as free house sites; free timber for their houses; free food for themselves and for their animals; free clothing; free dung for fuel, manure, and plastering the home; credit facilities; opportunities for supplementary employment; free use of tools and raw materials; casual leave; and aid in litigation.

This jajmani system of "interrelatedness in service" was an interrelatedness of unequals within the traditional caste hierarchy. As a result, relationships and transactions between members of the different jatis were "asymmetrical." This asymmetry, which affected Dalits most seriously, showed itself in a variety of ways. One was that some Dalit jatis received payments but no services from other jatis whom they served. For example, whereas the Bhangi would sweep for a Brahman jajman, no Brahman would perform priestly services for the Bhangis. No barber would cut the hair of either a Chamar or a Bhangi and no washerman would wash a Bhangi's clothes, although both received services from those whom they would not serve. Another form of asymmetry was that some forms of service were more dignified and others more unpleasant, degrading, or polluting to perform than others. It was, for example, far more dignified to give payments of food and clothing than to carry off dead animals. In like manner, some services were implicitly degrading to receive, such as the right to have left-over food from feasts from which one was otherwise excluded. A third asymmetry was that the system did not compensate all equally for services rendered but favored the high castes over the low. Dalits in particular were kept in poverty. With this inequality of rewards went an inequality of power. In cases of conflict over the fulfillment of jajmani obligations, the village panchayat (comprised of men from the dominant castes) invariably favored the higher caste patrons at the expense of their lower caste clients. This usually left the aggrieved client forced to accept his or her fate without further recourse. Wiser also pointed out that the asymmetries in the jajmani system had negative psychological consequences. This can be seen most graphically in his description of what the client had to do to get free timber, one of his important concessions, from his patron.

The "kam karnewala" usually gets the wood used in repair work by approaching his jajman in the attitude of a supplicant, as an inferior approaching a superior. He makes his request in a most submissive manner by bowing before the jajman with folded hands, touching his forehead. This posture is called "hath jhorke" which means literally folded hands. It is more dignified than begging, but involves a recognition of subserviency.[4]

In fact, it fostered a deferential attitude and even "slave mentality" among Dalits in the presence of their more favored jajmans.[5] These asymmetries in and consequences of the jajmani system reinforced rather than undermined the social hierarchy of the village as well as the practice of untouchability from which Dalits also suffered.

Yet, despite the inequalities, injustices, humiliations and bare subsistence existence that went with it, this system did offer the Dalits within it security. They had a house, a job, and a minimal livelihood. In the last analysis, the sense of security it offered was more powerful than the sense of grievance it engendered. Wiser found villagers very reluctant to move towards a more remunerative, voluntaristic and individualistic work system, either in cooperative farming or in the mills and factories, because the risks involved threatened the sense of security which the jajmani system offered.[6]

---

[4] *Ibid.*, 97.   The asymmetries in the jajmani system and the behavior it required of Dalit clients may explain the "uncalled-for insolence" which Barakat Ullah described in the previous chapter. *Infra*, 10-11.

[5] *Ibid.*, 174.

[6] "Villagers are loathe to give up their jajmani compensations and rights.   Occasionally one of them ventures to go to the city where he receives money wages more than equivalent to his income from the jajmani system.   He takes the cash, but feels injured when he finds that he is no longer entitled to the old perquisites. Furthermore, he is not able to spend so much money wisely.   When his wages stop, there is no place for him to fit in.   There are no more tragic figures in India than the unemployed who have no village home.   This love for the security of the village is the despair of mill and factory owners, because very few labourers are willing to settle permanently in a factory area. The security of the village community is its strength." *Ibid.*, 186.

Wiser wrote his pioneering work in 1932.[7] Village studies carried out about two decades later indicated that the jajmani system and the Dalits' place in it were not confined to North India. Moreover, there were indications from all over the country that contract was beginning to replace custom as the basis for these patron-client relationships.[8] M.N. Srinivas found in the Mysore village he studied that the traditional master-servant relationship prevalent before World War I was now a contract relationship, reinforced by tenancy and debtorship ties between client and patron.[9] In a Tanjore village at about the same time there were still some hereditary serfs; more common, however, was the Adi Dravida who had become "attached" to a Brahman landlord through indebtedness.[10] In a North Kerala village the Dalits had been serfs tied to a particular plot of land and many were still bound in traditional servant-master relationships.[11] Permanent "attached" relationships between Madigas and landlords also existed in the village within the former Hyderabad State S.C. Dube studied; however, it is not clear whether those were customary or contractual relationships.[12] Cohn, Kolenda, and Lewis all found the jajmani system still functioning in the North Indian villages they studied in the 1950s, although the latter indicated that several jatis, including the Chamars, had opted out of it.[13]

---

[7] *Ibid.*, 16. However, the book was published four years later.

[8] David G. Mandelbaum later argued that many of those relations thought to have been customary jajmani relations were in fact contractual anyway. *Society in India* (Bombay, 1972), 162.

[9] "The Social System of a Mysore Village," in McKim Marriott, ed., *Village India: Studies in the Little Community* (Chicago, 1955), 27.

[10] Kathleen Gough, "The Social Structure of a Tanjore Village," in M.N. Srinivas, ed., *India's Villages* (Revised edition; Bombay, 1960), 92.

[11] Eric J. Miller, "Village Structure in North Kerala," in *ibid.*, 45 & 52.

[12] *Indian Village* (Bombay, 1967), 68-69. This book was originally published in England in 1955.

[13] Bernard S. Cohn, "The Changing Status of a Depressed Caste," in McKim Marriott, ed., *op. cit.*, 55-56. Pauline Kolenda presented some of her earlier research on this subject in *Caste in Contemporary India: Beyond*

While jajmani relations were undergoing change in all of these villages studied in the 1950s, the disabilities Dalits suffered remained the same. They had to live either on the edge or completely outside of the village; they were not allowed to enter Brahman temples or use certain streets; they were also not allowed to use the village well or to bathe in the river upstream from where the higher castes bathed. They were expected to show deferential behavior and efforts to assert themselves were met with strong resistance. Finally, they were generally both addressed and treated with contempt by those above them in the village hierarchy.

Changes in the jajmani system, already apparent in the 1950s, had become even more obvious in the village studies carried out a decade or two later. Economic forces were largely responsible for the jajmani system's decline. The village's subsistence economy became increasingly integrated with the commercial economy of the region and nation. New agricultural technologies and cash crops were introduced. Land-holdings were fragmented as the population increased and village wastelands, where Dalits had the right to get wood and graze animals, began to disappear. Urban manufactured goods competed successfully with those made by village potters, goldsmiths, weavers, and leather-workers for their jajmans. Water-carriers were replaced by courtyard hand pumps. All of these changes made the services of Dalit menials easier to dispense with. Men began to migrate to the towns and cities to find more remunerative employment. Some Dalits gave up their traditional work because they now considered it too degrading. Earlier the jajmani system had provided even Dalits with a basic security; jajmans had to treat their Dalit clients with some degree of benevolent paternalism and clients believed "themselves to have a *right* to support from their agriculturalist jajmans." [14] Increasingly, status, political and especially economic considerations were now governing the largely contractual relations between patrons and clients. With this change has come mounting tension. Reported instances of inter-caste atrocities and

---

Organic Solidarity (Menlo Park, 1978), 46-51. Oscar Lewis, *Village Life in Northern India: Studies in a Delhi Village* (New York, 1965), 78-79. This book was originally published in 1958.

[14] This important phrase is taken from Pauline Kolenda, *op. cit.,* 48.

communal violence have become more frequent in the villages.[15] Apart from a longing for stability and a desire to hold on to what was good and necessary in the old order, what seems to hold Dalit clients and their patrons together in the village today is the dominant caste patrons' economic and coercive power as well as their Dalit clients' abject economic dependency and lack of viable alternatives.[16]

THE URBAN SETTING

Prior to the advent of British rule, the social structure of Indian towns and cities seems to have been very similar to that of the villages. Each jati or Muslim clan had its own traditional occupation and, among Hindus, these were ranked in a hierarchy of ritual purity and pollution. Moreover, members of the same jatis and clans tended to live together in the same urban neighborhoods and so share a common social life. However, the towns and cities were much larger than the villages and their economies were based upon commerce, industry, government, education and culture. As a result, the jatis and clans dominant in the urban centers were traditionally engaged in these activities rather than in agriculture. In fact, some trading jatis, like the Khatris in northwest India, were almost exclusively urban jatis. The Dalit jatis were at the bottom of the urban social hierarchy, doing much the same kind of work as in the villages: sweeping, leather work, weaving, basket or mat making, and the like.

The British introduced both an industrial revolution and a new cultural ethos into urban India. The result was greatly enhanced occupational diversity. The railways, mills, military, educational system and new professions created jobs for which there were no traditional castes (e.g., printer, mechanic, typist, nurse, railway

---

[15] See John C.B. Webster, *The Dalit Christians: A History*, 166-168.

[16] See two case studies from U.P. and Bihar as well as a survey of the literature on this general subject. Miriam Sharma, *The Politics of Inequality: Competition and Control in an Indian Village* (Honolulu, 1978); Dinesh Khosla, *Myth and Reality of the Protection of Civil Rights Law: A Case Study of Untouchability in Rural India* (Delhi, 1987); James M. Freeman, "The Consciousness of Freedom among India's Untouchables," in Dilip K. Basu and Richard Sisson, eds., *Social and Economic Development in India: A Reassessment* (New Delhi, 1986), 153-171.

brakeman, etc.) and Dalits were able to enter into some of these new occupations quite early. For example, in the Bombay Presidency the British recruited Mahars into their armies to fight against the Marathas at the turn of the last century. By the turn of this century Mahars were laborers working on the railways, in the mills, on the docks or with coal. Some entered domestic service with the British.[17] With these opportunities for occupational mobility came possibilities for education and dreams of even more personal and family mobility for the next generation. By Independence, the earlier identification of caste with occupation could no longer be assumed in the towns and cities. Social mobility through employment in the modern industrialized sector of the economy had changed that and made the social structure more complex, with a class structure overlying rather than replacing that of caste and clan. The Government of India enacted a reservation policy designed to help Dalits enhance their class status on the assumption that this would, in turn, enable them to interact with members of other castes on terms of greater equality.

The Dalits' more recent urban setting therefore combines the traditional and the modern. Unlike the rural setting, it is also segmented into several separate spheres, perhaps the two most important ones being the residential and the work environments. With regard to the former, most urban Dalits continue to live in neighborhoods with fellow members of their jatis. These mohallas or bastis are the centers of their social and communal lives. People belonging to other castes live elsewhere in other neighborhoods and enter the Dalit neighborhoods only occasionally. Owen Lynch has described one such neighborhood, "Bhim Nagar" in Agra, whose residents, while occupationally diverse, share a similar way of life and address each other in kinship terms.[18] Another, probably increasingly common type of residential area as the cities continue to grow, is "Chennanagar," a slum in northern Madras. This relatively new residential colony was begun on unoccupied municipal land in 1966. Of the 376 families living there when Paul Wiebe studied it in the early

---

17 Eleanor Mae Zelliot, "Dr. Ambedkar and the Mahar Movement" (Unpublished Ph. D. dissertation: University of Pennsylvania, 1969), 33-41.

18 Owen W. Lynch, *The Politics of Untouchability: Social Mobility and Social Change in a City of India* (Delhi, 1974), 166-202.

1970s, only 21 were Dalits.[19] Yet, in this "mixed" neighborhood, caste distinctions were not very important and there was "almost no ranking of the castes according to ritual purity."[20] One of the reasons for this was that "in the conditions of poverty in which the people find themselves, ritual purity is a matter of relatively little concern."[21] Instead only very general caste identifications were used: Brahmans and others or Dalits and others.[22] Residents of "Chennanagar" had relatively little to do with each other on a day to day basis and so caste prejudice seems to have had little impact there.[23] On the other hand, middle class urban Dalits seeking housing for their families outside Dalit neighborhoods have often been denied rental accommodation once the landlords discover that they are Dalits.[24]

Recent studies of the Dalits' urban workplace reveal a similar combination of continuity with and change from the past. Many urban Dalits have continued on in their traditional occupations. For example, in many North Indian cities Bhangis are employed as sweepers not just in private homes but more importantly by municipal committees and other government agencies, factories and banks, schools and hospitals. Jatavs and other Chamars have turned their leather-working skills to good advantage in the export-oriented shoe business. Some urban Dalits even continue to work within a patron-client relationship. Wiebe found what he called "fragments of the jajmani system" in

---

[19] Paul D. Wiebe, *Social Life in an Indian Slum* (Durham, 1975), 62.

[20] *Ibid.*, 65.

[21] *Ibid.*

[22] *Ibid.*, 68. About 85% of the residents were in the non-Brahman category in between.

[23] Sumati N. Dubey found, upon interviewing 540 randomly selected residents in some mixed housing colonies in Andhra Pradesh and Maharashtra, that the higher caste residents became less ethnocentric while the Dalits became more prejudiced against the higher castes as a result of living in the same neighborhood. Abstract of "Positive Discrimination and Ethnocentric Attitudes Among the Scheduled Castes," by J. Verma in *Indian Psychological Abstracts* (June 1981), 190.

[24] Harold R. Isaacs, *India's Ex-Untouchables* (Bombay, 1965), 135-136, 144-145.

Madras, especially but not exclusively among domestic servants in upper class residential neighborhoods.[25]   Karlekar found that the women of a sweeper colony in Delhi "owned" the right to clean specific houses in specific neighborhoods.[26] However, unlike municipal sweepers, they had few "rights;" instead, they seem to have been as much at the mercy of their employers as their rural counterparts were with regard to pay, leave, and such extras as clothes or gifts at festival times. Many were treated with persistent contempt ("like animals") and kept from the "clean" sections of the home. Municipal sweepers, on the other hand, were much better off; they had job security, regular pay, pensions, casual leave, uniforms, maternity benefits and the like.[27] Municipal sweepers were also unionized and so were apt to be treated better.[28]

However, it has been in the modern sector where the greatest opportunities for employment and mobility have opened up. Decent jobs have not been easy to get, the competition has been very stiff, and so unemployment as well as underemployment among Dalits is not uncommon. Yet, despite these difficulties, the occupational diversity among urban Dalits is considerable. The samples of two recent studies illustrate this diversity. S.M. Dahiwale's study of 230 self-employed Dalits in Kolhapur, Maharashtra shows 30 in their traditional occupations. The remaining 200 are in modern occupations: doctors, lawyers, chartered accountants, radio or watch repair, owners or workers in various kinds of engine manufacture and repair shops, transportation, selling eatables, cycle sales and repair, skilled construction work, painting, and tailoring.[29] Nandu Ram's sample of 240 Dalits drawn from the various cadres of central and state government employees in

25   Paul D. Wiebe, *op. cit.*, 92.

26   Malavika Karlekar, *Poverty and Women's Work: A Study of Sweeper Women in Delhi* (New Delhi, 1982), 92-93.

27   *Ibid.*, 79-101.

28   *Ibid*; Satish Saberwal, *Mobile Men: Limits to Social Change in Urban Punjab* (New Delhi, 1976), 62-63; Dr. Shyamlal, *Caste and Political Mobilization: The Bhangis* (Jaipur, 1981), 47-62.

29   S.M. Dahiwale, *Emerging Entrepreneurship Among Scheduled Castes Of Contemporary India: A Study of Kolhapur City* (New Delhi, 1989), 62-65.

Kanpur, U.P. included not only sweepers, peons, clerical and technical staff, but also supervisors as well as Class II and Class I officers.[30] In both cases the degree of occupational mobility from their fathers' and grandfathers' generations was impressive.

Has this kind of improvement in class status brought with it greater respect and better treatment from colleagues belonging to higher castes? In a pioneering study of this subject back in 1963, Harold Isaacs shared insights gained from stories told by 50 highly articulate Dalit informants. He described these modern urban Dalits as in a kind of "semi-limbo," well integrated with neither other middle class Indians nor the mass of their own people. Strong incentives existed to keep one's Dalit background a secret in the workplace. Old attitudes were not dead. Incompetence and the Scheduled Castes were often linked together in the popular imagination. Competition, stress and conflict could lead to open expression of degrading caste prejudice. Friendships with colleagues could be altered once one's caste was known. Consequently, some Dalits went to great lengths to hide their caste background. Others tried to lead a non-Dalit life in public while living a Dalit private and family life. Yet others have chosen neither to hide nor to advertize their caste. All faced the problem of what and how and when to tell their children about their caste. Most delayed saying anything about it so that their children would not develop a complex about it during their early years.[31]

Other, more recent studies have confirmed that while upwardly mobile urban Dalits do indeed enjoy greater respect and better social interaction with colleagues from other castes than was previously the case, there are limits to the progress they have made.[32] Indeed, although they feel little "status anxiety" about the contradictions between their class and caste status, they have probably achieved about all they feel they can expect to achieve in this respect. As a result, they do remain a somewhat separate and distinct group within the society at

---

[30] Nandu Ram, *The Mobile Scheduled Castes: Rise of a New Middle Class* (Delhi, 1988), 43.

[31] Harold R. Isaacs, *op. cit.,* 128-160.

[32] These are summarized in John C.B. Webster, *The Dalit Christians: A History,* 153-154.

large.[33]

THE PSYCHOLOGICAL SETTING

The Dalits' rural and urban settings have influenced not only their external circumstances but also their inner lives. Social scientists have described how these social environments have shaped not just Dalit behavior but Dalit thoughts and feelings as well. This section therefore begins by examining the nature and consequences of this kind of social conditioning. It then looks at some of the results of psychological research comparing Dalits and non-Dalits for the insights into the Dalit psyche those provide. Finally, an attempt will be made to relate these two types of data to each other in a meaningful synthesis.

The rural social setting described earlier seems to have affected the Dalit psyche in two important ways. For one thing, it has both instilled a sense of inherent inferiority in them and provoked their anger and resentment.

The inculcation of attitudes of inferiority may be seen in the everyday experience of the very young. It does not require much time for the Sweeper child accompanying his mother on her daily rounds to realize his position in society. The nature of the tasks performed by an Untouchable's parents, the mode of address and the tone of voice used by upper castes in issuing instructions, are readily apparent to children. The sending of Sweeper children to collect food left over from upper caste feasts, their receipt of "gifts" on inauspicious occasions such as the eclipse of the sun, and their "right" to the clothing of the dead--all serve to reaffirm their association with pollution and inferior status.[34]

This has led not only to the deferential behavior described by Wiser,[35] but also to the expressions of anger directed at patrons or each other

---

33   This is the conclusion of Nandu Ram which finds general support from other studies. *Op. cit.,* 90 & 120.

34   J. Michael Mahar, "Agents of Dharma in a North Indian Village," in J. Michael Mahar, ed., *The Untouchables in Contemporary India* (Tucson, 1972), 23.

35   *Infra.,* 28.

described by Barakat Ullah and Heinrichs.[36] More recent observers have also noted both tendencies, including a greater unwillingness among the younger generation to put up with the indignities of the past.[37] The rural social setting had also conditioned Dalits to feel both secure and dependent in their client-patron relationships.[38] With the decline of the jajmani system, the objective conditions which nurtured such feelings may have eroded, but Dalits may still carry over into changed circumstances a predisposition for dependent relationships in which they feel that they are owed support.

The psychological impact of the urban environment is less clear. However, it is likely that the kind of psychological impacts which village society has made upon Dalits provides the most fruitful starting point for understanding the social conditioning of the urban environment as well. The urban Dalit is either being shaped by the same social forces as the rural Dalit (especially if he/she is a recent migrant from a village) or else is struggling to be free from them. For example, Karlekar found among the sweeper women she interviewed in Delhi plenty of anger and resentment at the insulting treatment they had to put up with in the private homes where they worked.[39] R. S. Khare found the Chamars in Lucknow trying to deal very pragmatically with issues of self-image, education, health, housing, and livelihood so as to

---

[36] *Infra.*, 10-13.

[37] Bernard S. Cohn, *op. cit.*, 61; Joan P. Mencher, "Continuity and Change in an Ex-Untouchable Community of South India," in J. Michael Mahar, ed., *op. cit.*, 48-49. In his biography of Muli, a Dalit from a village in Orissa, James M. Freeman writes, "Muli expected to be insulted, avoided, and cheated in his everyday contact with higher-caste people, and he retaliated by cheating them. Muli delighted in expressing self-deprecatory statements to a high-caste person precisely when he knew that that person desperately needed his help and would willingly deny the conventional high-caste stereotype that Muli was a pollutant. Muli, however, repeated the theme of his pollution numerous times, leaving the impression that he had internalized the very norms that he ridiculed. His own self-image was shaped by the very oppression that he rejected." *Untouchable; An Indian Life History* (Stanford, 1979), 383-384.

[38] See William Wiser's comments, *infra.*, 28; also Pauline Kolenda, *op. cit.*, 48 and J. Michael Mahar, *op. cit.*, 25.

[39] Malavika Karlekar, *op. cit.*, 84-85, 88.

reduce the institutionalized disabilities from which they have suffered. The tendencies he discerned among them to undo the effects of social conditioning were:
(a) holding *thers* primarily responsible for their social stresses and deprivations; (b) criticizing their own low social estimates of themselves; (c) translating social subordination (and their "innate inferiority") into a confrontation of cultural ideologies, and the latter into a contest of pragmatic and political tactics; (d) raising a positive accountability for themselves under a secular democratic ethos; (e) multiplying practical and political arenas in which to test new provisions of their rights against traditional responsibilities; (f) campaigning for stronger government support and protection to quickly right accumulated deprivations; and (g) seeking to reconstitute their identity and individuation so totally that they become culturally genuine and unconditional recipients of social equality and justice.[40]

In order to complement analyses of social conditioning by looking at the inner world of Dalits more directly, the *Indian Psychological Abstracts* from 1972 to 1990 were surveyed. The number of studies specifically on Dalits found there was very small. Moreover, all of them seem to have been conducted in North India, generally with student samples. The earliest and probably most seminal of these was that carried out by Prem Shanker in 1951. Shanker administered Rorschach tests to 20 male Dalit college students and 20 uneducated male Dalits selected at random from a list of municipal employees who were similar in age and income to the educated group. Those findings were compared with general Indian norms developed a decade later to see how the Dalit sample varied from the Indian population as a whole. This comparison showed that Dalits were below the general norm in intelligence, sociability, and ego strength; they were above the norm in anxiety, impulsiveness, immaturity, neurotic and psychotic tendencies. Within the Dalit sample the educated were more intelligent, ambitious, anxious, passive, egocentric, emotionally immature, withdrawn, inhibited, and evasive in their responses than the uneducated. There were also more signs of neurosis and failure in social adjustment among the educated, while the uneducated showed greater dependency need and fear of a destructive father image. Equally significant was the finding

---

40   *The Untouchable as Himself: Ideology, Identity and Pragmatism among the Lucknow Chamars* (Cambridge, 1984), 135.

that even though they "show more uncontrollable and raw emotions and impulses," Dalits revealed no more inferiority feelings than were found in the Indian population as a whole. This Shanker attributed to the fact that a negative self-image had been imposed upon the Dalits from outside themselves and was not inherent within them.[41]

Many of Shanker's findings have been supported by subsequent studies which have employed different research instruments. These findings about Dalits include lower intelligence, more frustration, neuroticism, anxiety and depression. However, in 1977 M.K. Hassan conducted a study of college students in urban Bihar which, while agreeing with most of Shanker's findings, contradicted the finding about Dalit self-image. Hassan found the Dalits (and Scheduled Tribes) had a more negative self-image as well as higher degrees of anxiety, authoritarianism, and dependence proneness as well as a lower need for achievement than did the high or low caste students. In fact, their negative self-image showed a stronger correlation with these other concomitant tendencies than did negative self-images among other students.[42] Both Shanker's and Hassan's contradictory findings about Dalit self-image have found support from subsequent studies and Hassan's finding about greater authoritarianism among Dalits has also been both supported and contradicted in later research.

In the mid-1980s three psychologists in Kanpur carried out similar research among fifty lower middle class boys between the ages of 14 and 18 years old. Half of these intermediate college students were Dalits and half were from higher castes. The personality inventory showed statistically significant differences between the two groups at four of its nine points. The Dalits scored lower on empathy, need to achieve, and dogmatism, but much higher on pessimism. This last trait the authors saw as a sign of a continuing sense of insecurity. Yet, despite this difference, the Dalits' scores on ego ideal and self-confidence were not significantly different from those of the higher caste respondents. What gives this study special significance, however, is that it is set within a theoretical framework derived from studies of oppressed and marginalized groups in other societies. Such groups

[41] Prem Shanker, "Education and Rorschach Affective Factors of the Harijans," *Indian Psychological Review,* 4 (January,1968), 96-100.

[42] Abstract of Hassan, M.K. "Social Deprivation, Self-Image and Some Personality Traits," by M. Jain in *Indian Psychological Abstracts* (June 1978), 109.

elsewhere have also been found to exhibit low self-esteem, confusion about their identity, self-hate, a perception of the world as a hostile place, hypertension, neuroticism, and low intellectual development. Thus these traits appear to be not uniquely Dalit traits, but traits more universally manifested by similarly situated peoples. Moreover, the authors point out that scores on intelligence tests are indicators not of innate inferiority but of cultural deprivation.[43]

It is undoubtedly dangerous to draw firm conclusions about the Dalit psyche on the basis of occasionally contradictory studies of very small samples of young Dalits in one part of the country. Yet these findings, when taken in conjunction with those on social conditioning described earlier, do seem to fit a pattern. Psychologically, the rural setting has been and continues to be demeaning and aggravating for Dalits. It has discouraged initiative and achievement among them, but has until fairly recently rewarded dependency with some security, thus at least partially satisfying what is perhaps the deepest need (the need to survive) of the socially and economically marginalized Dalits. Given the almost total decline of the jajmani system in the villages with nothing comparably secure to replace it, as well as the absence of anything offering similar security in the towns and cities, one can understand why Dalits might be unusually anxious, uncertain, socially maladjusted, impulsive, self-absorbed, and emotionally dependent upon real or potential patrons. This would be especially true of Dalit students who are in the highly vulnerable position of attempting to make a major transition from the more traditional world of their parents to the new, largely unknown, more modern culture of the towns and cities they hope to work in. Whether or not they have a negative self-image, they still have to contend with the negative public image of their own people. To date the socio-cultural supports (and even the government reservation system) are not strong enough to carry Dalits through such a transition confidently and serenely in the face of continuing caste prejudice. Those supports for a fundamental reorientation of life will take time to build.

---

43 K.S. Senger, S.B. Singh, and A.K. Srivastava, "Personality Traits of Scheduled and non Scheduled Caste Adolescents: A Comparative Study," *Child Psychiatry Quarterly* 18 (1985), 2:48-52. This study also provides a useful summary of the findings of previous studies on this subject (p. 49).

THE ECCLESIASTICAL SETTING

Ecclesiastical settings vary greatly according to denominational tradition and location within India. Rather than attempting to describe all of these variations here, this section will be confined to a description of just one setting, the Madras diocese of the Church of South India, since that provided the specific setting in which data was collected for this study. At present the Madras diocese is spread along the coast of the Bay of Bengal north from the city of Madras into the Nellore district of Andhra Pradesh and south into Pondicherry. It extends inland into the southern tip of Chitoor district in Andhra Pradesh as well as into some of the eastern part of South Arcot district in Tamilnadu. Small portions of Andhra Pradesh were included in the Madras diocese because the Protestants there happen to speak Tamil rather than Telugu.

This area had been evangelized by the Methodist Missionary Society, the Church of Scotland Mission, and the American Arcot Mission (Reformed Church of America). The area around Madras was a mass movement area where, beginning in the late nineteenth century, Dalits converted to Christianity in large numbers. This has given the diocese its particular character. The churches outside the metropolitan area are overwhelmingly Dalit, whereas the social composition of those in Madras itself is much more mixed. They are made up of long time Madras residents as well as migrants not only from the surrounding towns and villages but also from as far away as Madurai, Tinnevelly, and Kerala.

The churches to which these three missions were related, as well as the Anglican churches in the city of Madras, merged into the Church of South India when it was inaugurated in Madras on September 27, 1947. Since then the diocese has had only five bishops, the most recent of whom is the Rt. Rev. Masilamani Azariah who was consecrated on January 2, 1990. The diocese is now divided into four areas, two of which (Madras North and Madras South) are within the city of Madras itself. As the statistics on pastorates and membership in Table 1 indicate, the diocese is overwhelmingly urban. Just over sixty percent of all baptized Christians, 66.2% of all the communicants, 62.9% of the families, and 65.3% of the pastorates are in Madras itself. In addition, there are several large towns or small cities in the Southern and Central Areas of the diocese which have urban congregations as well. Whereas the congregations in Madras are, on the average, larger

TABLE 1

CENSUS OF THE MADRAS DIOCESE AS OF APRIL 1, 1992

	Total	Madras North	Madras South	Central Area	Southern Area
Pastorates	118	40	37	22	19
Congregations	656	92	64	320	180
Families	43,994	14,976	12,708	9,765	6,545
Communicants	90,406	33,994	25,859	15,515	15,038
Baptized Christians	140,304	48,941	36,529	32,472	22,362

Source: Diocese of Madras, Church of South India: Appendix to the Statistical Review for 1993.

than those outside it (384 vs. 76 communicants per congregation), the average number of congregations per pastorate is much smaller (two vs. ten). Thus the pastoral load is actually distributed quite evenly. Each pastor (presbyter) in charge of a pastorate in Madras has an average of 777 communicant members in his/her care, while those outside have an average of 745. During 1993-94 the diocese created 26 new pastorates either by dividing existing ones or by adding new ones.[44] It also built 26 new churches, 18 of which are in pastorates outside Madras.[45] Since these increases in pastorates and church buildings are signs of growth, the number of communicants each pastor is responsible for remains high.

[44] Church of South India, Diocese of Madras, *Draft Reports of The Madras Diocesan Council 1995*, 16B.

[45] *Ibid.*, 29-30. However, lest this appear to reflect an unwarranted rural bias, it should be borne in mind that three-quarters of the actual costs of new church construction was actually devoted to the eight Madras churches.

Pastors within the diocese are assigned their pastorates by the bishop instead of being called by members of the pastorates and, according to diocesan rules, pastors must be transferred after serving a pastorate for five years. Pastors are paid from diocesan funds according to scales set by the diocese itself and for this purpose the pastorates are assessed fixed amounts to pay into a central fund. Thus, in effect, all the pastorates share in the support of all the clergy rather than each one supporting only its own pastor. Power is thus centralized in the diocese and its committees, on which both pastors and lay people serve. Centralization has had its benefits for the conduct of ministry. For example, the diocese has made provision for pastors to purchase motorcycles or scooters so that they may visit their parishes and parishioners more easily. This is of special help to rural pastors whose parishes are scattered in areas where public transportation is infrequent, but all pastors have benefitted from the arrangement. Rural pastors are also assisted by catechists, Bible women, and village health guides paid by the diocese.[46] In urban parishes catechists are less common. Instead, lay volunteers often work with the pastor in carrying out a wide variety of pastoral responsibilities. The diocese also runs a large number of schools, some hospitals and other institutions, as well as some special projects and programs within its boundaries. These provide both resources pastors can draw upon and constituencies they must serve in ministry.

At the local level the pastor works with a pastorate committee elected by the voting members of the pastorate. Together they exercise oversight of the worship, ministry and mission of the parishes within the pastorate. These pastorate committees enjoy considerable autonomy within their own spheres of jurisdiction. When, however, they need more money than they can raise locally to carry out a project which has become a priority for them, they must apply to the diocese for assistance and thus make their project subject to diocesan scrutiny and evaluation.

Being a pastor to Dalits within the Madras diocese of the Church of

---

[46] The catechists actually serve in an honorary capacity but are given a gift from the diocese at the end of the year. The village health guides are young women from the villages who have completed ten years of schooling and then receive special training for one month at the C.S.I. hospital in Ikkadu. At the end of 1994 there were village health guides in thirty pastorates. *Ibid.,* 120-123.

South India means functioning within these kinds of structures which provide an institutional framework and discipline for pastoral ministry. However, the focus of this study will be upon the pastor's relationship not to the institutional framework itself but to the Dalit parishioners within that same framework. That is why the social and psychological setting of Dalit parishioners is of greater significance here than is the ecclesiastical setting. Where the ecclesiastical setting becomes especially important is in establishing and implementing specific pastoral priorities, for these have to be determined and carried out with the constraints of a particular Christian tradition, a particular ecclesiastical structure, as well as with particular amounts and kinds of available human or other resources very much in mind.

CHAPTER 3

PASTORS' PERCEPTIONS

Perception is crucial to pastoral ministry. What the pastor has "eyes to see and ears to hear" about his/her people, the world they live in, their needs, mind-set, psychology and life style, as well as about the work of God in the complexity and totality of their lives, will affect the pastor's ministry with them. At the same time, perception also provides insights into the workings of the pastor's own mind which processes data from "out there" on the basis of personal past experience and assumptions about that data.[1] This chapter therefore examines the perceptions of pastors to Dalits in order to understand both the pastors themselves and their pastoral situations. Five questions guide the inquiry. Who are these people and how did they become pastors? What are their particular pastoral assignments and responsibilities? What kinds of Dalits are they pastors to? How do they perceive their pastoral situations and how do they minister to the Dalits in those situations? What kinds of results do they believe these ministries have produced, and not produced? The chapter begins with a collective portrait of the Madras pastors, treats their rural and urban ministries separately, and then compares them with the Batala pastors before arriving at some conclusions.

THE PASTORS

There is no one pastor who is "typical" or "representative" of them all. However, a brief biography does provide a useful introduction to the collective portrait which will follow. From the days of his childhood Y.L. Babu Rao had wanted to be a pastor. He grew up in a Tamil-speaking Dalit family in Andhra Pradesh where his father worked as a peon for the Public Works Department. However, when he was still quite young, Babu Rao left home so that he might study in Tamil, his mother tongue, rather than in Telugu, the medium of instruction

---

[1] Here it is assumed that perception of such complex phenomena as human beings within their contexts is not a direct process but a constructed process guided by past experience and involving one's own assumptions and cognitive powers.

where his father worked. He went to live first in the suburbs of Madras with his uncle, who was a C.S.I. catechist and teacher, and then in the C.S.I. hostel in Tirullavur. After completing a B.A. in economics from Voorhees College in Vellore, he approached the Madras diocese for sponsorship as a candidate for the ministry. At that time he was told to either get a job or study further as he was not yet ready. He applied again two years later after completing an M.A. in philosophy at Madras Christian College. This time he was accepted. He was sent first to work under the pastor at Rayapuram in Madras as a probationer and then to United Theological College in Bangalore for his B.D. studies. Upon graduation in 1981 he served first a rural and then a suburban/rural pastorate. While at his second pastorate he was married to a teacher and their daughter was born. For the past five years he has served an urban pastorate. In June 1995 he will be transferred to his fourth pastorate. Since his days as a probationer in Rayapuram, Babu Rao has been a musician and singer who has composed songs for worship. In recent years he has developed new liturgies for special occasions as well. Currently he serves as Director of the Madras Diocese's Department of Communication.

Babu Rao first became aware of Dalit issues as a child when he returned home from Madras and Tirullavur for his vacations. There, as part of a poor family, he experienced the caste divisions and discrimination which he had not experienced while living in his uncle's home or at school. Later, when at United Theological College, he gained further clarity on these issues while carrying out field research in his native place for a course on "Christianity and the Depressed Classes Movement." The other important influence on his thinking after he became a pastor in the Madras diocese was the Rev. M. Azariah, who was then General Secretary of the Church of South India.[2]

The Rev. Babu Rao fits well into the collective portrait of the Madras pastors. All but one of them are Dalits. All but one are men and all but one Lutheran are presbyters in the Madras diocese of the Church of South India. They range in age from 30 to 54, with an average age of 40, and have been ordained for between two and nineteen years. A few are in their first pastorates and there are a few who are now in their fifth or sixth pastorates. They are an unusually well educated group. All of

---

2 M. Azariah's role as a pioneer in Dalit Christian liberation is described in John C.B. Webster, *The Dalit Christians: A History*, 192, 231-232, 238-239.

them have a Bachelor of Divinity (B.D.) degree. Ten have other post-graduate degrees as well (six M.A., two B. Ed., and two M.S.W.) and four have studied abroad (two in the U.K., one in the U.S.A., and one in both the U.S.A. and Korea). All but one are married, several to spouses from castes considered higher than their own.

Their backgrounds are somewhat more diverse than are their professional training or present circumstances. They are almost evenly divided between those from urban and those from rural backgrounds. Their parents' occupations were somewhat varied. While eight are children of teachers and two of pastors, the parents of the others were pharmacists (2), executives (2), a government employee, a factory worker, and a farmer.[3] About half were dedicated to the ministry by their parents. For about two-thirds the ministry has been their only full-time work since completing their B.A. or M.A. degree. One was an electrician until a family crisis led him into the ministry. Another was a government accountant who was drawn towards the ministry through active involvement in his congregation's youth group, choir, and Sunday School as well as in Youth for Christ. Four had been working for the Madras diocese in various lay capacities (school hostel warden, social worker, church worker among rural Dalit women and children, director of youth and then communications work) before receiving a theological education for work as pastors.

One of the most striking features of this sample is that almost all the pastors from urban backgrounds are currently serving urban pastorates, while almost all the pastors from rural backgrounds are serving rural pastorates. This might suggest that the clergy of the diocese are divided either into "urban track" and "rural track" categories or even along class lines. That, however, is unlikely because the rural pastors happen to be both younger (33 vs. 45 years old) and less experienced (4 vs. 12 years) on the average than are the urban pastors. Moreover, most of the urban pastors, like the Rev. Babu Rao, have had rural pastoral experience and some of the rural pastors have had urban pastoral experience, at least during their probationary period. The coincidence of family background and current assignment may be of benefit to their ministries, especially if they have had a contrasting pastoral experience before returning to pastor in the environment within which they grew up.

According to both their own self-assessment and that of a group of

---

[3] I do not have parental occupation data on the other two respondents.

Dalit Christians in each parish visited, this group of pastors has a diversity of special gifts including a strong personal discipline of prayer and Bible study, a passion for justice, motivational skills, organizing ability, rapport with youth, good preaching and teaching ability. Some pastors and Dalit parishioners emphasized learned skills while others emphasized such inner qualities as courage, commitment, faith, and humility; some mentioned important activities the pastor did well while others referred to good relationships the pastor had built up. There were some differences between the gifts which the pastors saw in themselves and the gifts which their Dalit parishioners saw and valued in them, but there were no signs of serious contradictions between the two. Several pastors were surprised to learn that their parishioners valued the energy of youth they bring to their ministries! There were no differences in the assessment of personal gifts between either urban and rural or older and younger pastors as a whole. Special gifts for ministry do not appear to be sociologically determined or even sociologically "called forth."

Having said that, it is important to note that there was a highly significant consensus concerning one shared characteristic which all of these pastors have. This is an ability to "move with people" of all kinds, and especially with Dalits. This expression points not only to such traits as natural friendliness, empathy, a willingness to listen and to speak sincerely, but also to such activities as visiting congregation members in their homes, coming when needed, and making genuine efforts to help people. Testimony to both the importance and the prevalence of this characteristic comes from the pastors themselves and especially from the Dalit parishioners interviewed. In fact, it appears to this observer to be absolutely indispensable for effective ministry to Dalits. A pastor who does not "move with Dalits," take a genuine interest in their well-being or really listen to them, does not visit them in their homes or receive food and drink from their hands, has no ministry among them, no matter how well that pastor preaches, prays, teaches and advocates for social justice.

THE RURAL PASTORATE

In each of the eight rural pastorates in this sample there is one pastor who is responsible for between ten and nineteen village congregations or parishes. These parishes are combined together for purposes of government under a single pastorate committee chaired by the pastor.

The pastor lives in a town or large village, but can reach any of his rural parishes by motorcycle within about 45 minutes. For example, one pastorate has one parish with 34 families (25 of whom are Dalit) in the town where the pastor lives, as well as 12 rural parishes with from five to 46 families in each one. Almost every parish has its own catechist to assist the pastor. In addition there may be a local Bible woman and a village health guide who receive a stipend from the diocese to work either in a cluster of villages or in the pastorate as a whole.

The pastors have three major responsibilities which take up most of their time and energy. The first of these is worship. Pastors generally conduct services in each parish once a month. In addition, while occasionally attending prayer meetings and healing services, the pastor conducts many special services for such rites of passage as birth, engagement, marriage, moving to a new house, and death. Visiting congregation members in their homes is a second responsibility. Unless there is a serious problem to discuss, these visits are normally quite brief, consisting of inquiries about the well-being of the family members, perhaps some pastoral advice, and a parting prayer. Each family in each parish is generally visited in this way at least once a year. Finally, there is the responsibility of providing guidance and counsel for those who seek it. The range of problems pastors are asked to address is considerable, ranging from the personal psychological-spiritual, to advice on education and/or employment, to political problems in dealing with landowners and the police. Some pastors mention evangelism, teaching, and administration as time-consuming as well, but worship, visitation and guidance are the three core activities of the rural pastor. The local catechist assists the pastor in the first two, but not much in the third.

Each pastor was asked to provide some statistical data on only one parish within their pastorate. These statistics provide a useful starting point for understanding the pastoral situation of the rural pastor to Dalits. All eight parishes selected for this purpose are quite old; the newest ones were begun about fifty years ago. The number of Christian families in these parishes range from twenty to eighty. In five of the eight parishes all the families are Dalits; in the three others all but one, two, or three families respectively are Dalits. Thus the rural parish is socially very homogeneous. It is located in the cheri so that all of the Christians' neighbors are also Dalits. In only one village were all the Dalits Christians; in the remainder, Christians comprised from ten to eighty percent of the Dalit population. The average comes to about forty percent, but is significantly higher in the three villages where the total Dalit population is less than one hundred families (80%) than in the five where is exceeds one hundred families (15%).

Economically as well as socially these parishes are quite homogeneous. In five of the villages at least 75% of the Christians are agricultural laborers and in two more over 90% are daily wage laborers in agriculture, construction, or biri-making. In these seven villages anywhere from 30% to 98% (about 75% on the average) are classified as "poor, or without steady income." In one village near Madras the percentage is lower because the people are employed in basically urban occupations. In three of the villages the majority of Christians are illiterate; in the others the largest percentage have only a primary education. In all but one of the parishes there is at least one Christian who is a college graduate. In the village where all the Dalits are Christians, they have organized a union to represent them in negotiating with the government for various rural development projects; however, the union has not yet attempted to bargain collectively with the landowners over wages for agricultural labor.

Given this picture of the rural parish, it should not be surprising that the pastors answered the question, "In this parish what do you consider to be the three most serious needs of the Dalit Christians?" in terms of changes in the outward circumstances of their parishioners' lives rather than in terms of changed patterns of behavior, a different outlook on life, or even in such religious terms as being "born again" and experiencing the liberating or healing power of Christ. For example, in response to a later interview question, all of the pastors acknowledged that alcoholism was a serious problem among rural Dalit Christians and that in many cases it led to wife-beating and child abuse. (This is not to say that all rural Dalit Christian men are alcoholics; the estimates ran from ten or twenty percent to "a lot.") However, to these pastors habitual over-consumption of alcohol was not a root cause of the Dalit Christians' problems, but a response to the harsh realities of their lives which did have the effect of exacerbating their problems. The root causes instead were three major circumstances of rural Dalit Christian life: the limited opportunities for regular gainful employment which might enable them to work their way out of poverty; their lack of education, or of appropriate education (i.e., learning a marketable skill or just becoming more politically and economically "aware"), which decreased their chances of rising out of poverty; and their lack of social status as Dalits within the wider village community.

It was in answer to the question, "What do you consider to be the two greatest difficulties in being a pastor to Dalits?" that habits of mind and, perhaps, behavior patterns begin to appear. There was no consensus on this question. Most of the answers did cluster around the pastor's inability to meet the needs for employment, education and status mentioned above. But their replies also included references to difficulties in uniting and organizing their parishioners, in meeting unrealistic expectations, in dealing with limited understanding, low self-esteem or unwillingness to change. The same was true in the pastoral assessments of the strengths of these parishes. While such external factors as the age of the church, good local leadership, a large concentration of Christians in one village, or the presence of some educated Christians were listed as strengths, so were such inner qualities and behavior patterns as unity (2), generous giving (2), hard work, militancy, faith, spirituality, interest in evangelism, as well as social and political awareness.

Four components of rural ministry emerge from the pastors' answers to questions about the ways in which they exercise leadership and work with these Dalit congregations while carrying out their major responsibilities. The first and most frequently mentioned of these is "moving with the people." As indicated earlier, this combines an open, friendly, and concerned presence with such behavior as regular visitation and efforts to "solve" the problems people bring. The second is preaching and teaching. This includes not only conducting regular services and classes but also developing special programs designed to meet specific Dalit needs. The third consists of less structured discussion, outside the context of worship, with groups and individuals about matters affecting the lives of the congregation and *cheri* community. Since Dalits often expect the pastor to "do it all," which increases not only the pastor's burden but also the Dalits' dependency, the fourth consists of sharing leadership with local Dalits, as well as encouraging their ideas and decisions.

In the pastors' assessment the results of this kind of ministry have been helpful to Dalits in increasing their unity, discipline, giving, witnessing, "awareness," and confidence. In short, it has enhanced the value of the Church and its gospel in Dalit eyes. It has also helped some Dalit Christians with a number of their immediate problems. However, it has not really improved their economic condition or provided adequate educational or employment opportunities for them. Whether that is because the Church is "passive to their needs" or because it simply lacks the resources to bring about significant change is a matter of debate. Probably both are true.

The Batala pastors' perceptions were in most respects similar to these. The Batala pastors saw both the Dalit Christian demand for certificates qualifying them for Scheduled Caste benefits from the government and addiction to alcohol and drugs as more serious problems for ministry than did the Madras pastors. However, the most pronounced difference between the two was that the rural congregations in the Punjab appear to live in a more highly charged political atmosphere than do those in Tamilnadu. The Batala pastors saw the Punjabi Christians' current politics and relations with landowners as confrontational. While the rural pastors there are caught up in this ongoing political struggle, those in Tamilnadu see themselves trying to instill in their Dalit parishioners the kind of "awareness" needed both for more advantageous resolutions of local conflicts and for participation in the broader Dalit struggle for justice, equality, and respect.

In a general discussion of pastoral ministry to rural Dalits, the pastors commented that rural Dalits see their pastor as "the head of the family" and as a "problem-solver and overseer." The two images are really one in substance, even if different in tone. They are images attached to a role rather than to the unique qualities of individuals who play that role. The pastors understand that and carry out their ministries within that definition of their role. But there is a tension between the problem-solving role they have been assigned by their parishioners in particular and the role which they see themselves called to play. Part of the tension arises from the pastors' inability to solve endless problems arising from the very nature of a village economy and social structure which the pastor cannot change. However, it is also due to the pastors' desire to educate their people in such a way that they would be equipped to define and solve their individual and collective problems more effectively on their own, instead of expecting the pastor to "do it all."

THE URBAN PASTORATE

The urban pastorate presents a marked contrast to the rural pastorate. Whereas the latter is characterized by a high degree of homogeneity, the former exhibits a high degree of diversity, due in part to the fact that the city is changing at a much faster rate than are the "interior" villages in particular. In this sample of eleven urban pastorates, there are three pastorates which are well over one hundred years old and three which have been developed since the 1950s in response to the rapid growth of new neighborhoods in the city of Madras. Most of them are what might be termed "neighborhood churches," drawing their membership from the section of the city in which the church itself is located. At least two pastorates, however, have a very long history and family ties with it draw people from greater distances to be together for worship on Sunday mornings. Although Tamil is the language generally used for worship, several congregations do have English services and one has a tradition of worshipping only in English.

Whereas virtually all the members in the rural pastorates are Dalits, the urban pastorates have a more socially diverse membership. In the ten urban pastorates for which statistics are available, the percentage of Dalit members ranges from a mere 7.8% to 98%. In five of these parishes Dalits are in a clear majority and in four others they are in a clear minority. Taken together, Dalits make up almost 60% of these parishes' 4350 members. All the parishes are located in socially diverse neighborhoods with large numbers of Dalits in them.

Within these parishes, the Dalit members are themselves very diverse. In two of them 75% of the Dalit members are graduates or post-graduates working either as professionals, as government servants, or with private companies. In another, 30% are graduates and 45% are secondary school matriculates; in two more, 70% or more are matriculates. At the bottom of the scale, in two parishes 72% and 40% of the Dalit members respectively are illiterate, while in a third the majority of Dalit Christians have only a primary education. The predominant occupations of Dalit members are equally diverse. Industrial workers make up 50%, 60% and 70% of the Dalits in three congregations; professionals comprise 50% and teachers 60% of the Dalit members of two parishes. In two parishes about one-third of the Dalit members are clerks. One pastor estimated that 40% of the Dalit members in his parish were Class IV government servants and another estimated that 50% of the Dalit members were coolies. To sum up, in their pastor's estimation, one is a parish in which Dalits are predominantly (70%) poor, in five parishes Dalits are predominantly (40-75%) working class, in three they are predominantly (50-70%) middle class, and in one the classes are fairly evenly divided.

The form of the urban pastorate also stands in striking contrast to that of the rural pastorate. Among these eleven pastorates, there is one which consists only of one city congregation. In several, two or three urban parishes have been combined into one pastorate or the pastor serves two small, single-parish pastorates simultaneously. Several urban churches have started up rural congregations with whom they are combined in a single pastorate, and in two cases town parishes have been combined with ten rural parishes each to form pastorates, as was the case with the town congregation in the rural sample. Half of the urban pastors have no catechists to assist them. Three have only one each, one has four and the pastors with ten rural parishes have ten and twelve each. One pastor is himself an assistant pastor in his pastorate.

Yet, despite all of this diversity within and among the urban pastorates, there is a consensus about the urban pastor's responsibilities. Like the rural pastor, the urban pastor devotes a lot of time to conducting worship services. However, since the urban pastor has fewer parishes to serve, he/she conducts services more frequently in each one than does the rural pastor. A second responsibility is house and hospital visitation. However, the time which rural pastors devote to counselling and problem-solving, the urban pastors devote to preparing for and conducting a large number of meetings: Bible studies, prayer meetings, fellowship groups, committees, youth groups, etc. Several pastors also mentioned working in the evangelistic and social service ministries which their congregations have undertaken. In addition, many have important diocesan responsibilities outside their pastorates. Some spend time interpreting diocesan policies to congregation members as well as to mediating between their congregations and the diocese when conflicts over policy and property matters arise.

Like their rural counterparts, the urban pastors saw the most important needs of their Dalit parishioners primarily in terms of changes in the external circumstances of their lives. Employment opportunities, education and housing were on almost every pastor's list. In his presentation to the consultation, the pastor of a working class congregation pointed out that in one parish in his pastorate, when educationally qualified Dalit Christian youth fail to get jobs, they usually end up wasting their time, becoming addicts, and selling their services as goondas in exchange for money to feed their addictions. Apart from these frustrated young people, however, alcoholism is not a problem among urban Dalit Christians, but handling money (for those who have it) is a problem. The pastor of a middle class congregation stated in his presentation that urban Dalit Christians tend to spend rather than to save, e.g., for a daughter's marriage or for the education of grandchildren. As a result, they need help in budgeting and financial planning.

However, for this pastor, the greatest problem confronting urban Dalit Christians remains their own caste background. This they often go to great lengths to hide, something which would be impossible in a village but which the anonymity and impersonality of the city make possible. Hiding in this way is more common within congregations in which Dalits are only a minority than in those in which they comprise a significant majority. In the former case, Dalits tend to be passive participants and rarely come forward as leaders lest their backgrounds become known. They also become reluctant to mingle with other Dalit Christians and even cut themselves off from poor relatives back in the village for the same reason. Some give and receive dowries, which is contrary to Dalit Christian custom; those who do marry outside their caste generally are most reluctant to affirm their Dalit origins. The other pastors agreed. To quote one who did not yet know who the Dalits were in the pastorate to which he had recently been assigned because they were hiding their backgrounds so well, "they need to feel proud instead of ashamed about themselves and about their roots."

In fact, virtually all of the urban pastors listed low Dalit self-esteem and the Dalit desire to hide their Dalit origins not only as the greatest obstacles pastors face in ministering to Dalit Christians but also as the chief difficulty Dalit Christians face in becoming what God intends them to be. It also affects the unity of Dalit Christians, which several pastors mentioned as one of their greatest needs. (Whether this is because low self-esteem and shame produce the kind of anti-social behavior which makes unity difficult or whether they merely prevent Dalit Christians from seeking out and identifying others in the same predicament was not made clear.) This is tragic because the pastors certainly recognize the potential of urban Dalit Christians, having found them to be faithful, generous, prayerful, supportive, cooperative, and capable of providing good leadership in the church.

This problem of low self-esteem and shame raises what is perhaps the most perplexing issue faced by the pastor to urban Dalits. How does one minister to Dalits when, on the one hand, they do not want to be openly identified as Dalits and, on the other, publicly addressing Dalit problems (e.g., in a sermon) can provoke a negative reaction from non-Dalit members which could place the unity of the congregation in jeopardy? The standard method of dealing with this dilemma has been a tacit understanding to keep quiet about it, for to discuss it openly is to "introduce caste into the church." This conspiracy of silence about caste and its adverse effects upon Dalits, to which all are party, makes ministry to Dalits in a mixed congregation highly problematical indeed.

There are two ways in which urban pastors deal with this dilemma, apart from providing what help they can on a personal basis. There is a very strong consensus among urban pastors about sharing decision-making with the lay leadership of the pastorate, and especially with the pastorate committee. This entails a lot of listening, a lot of flexibility, a lot of openness, and a lot of personal consultation with individual leaders. One pastor said that he does not push his own agenda but allows the pastorate committee to think about issues in terms of "the growth of the congregation and of the people." Another said that a lot of pastoral stroking, both positive and negative, was necessary. One form of stroking used by many pastors was giving credit for positive accomplishments to the lay people involved rather than taking it for oneself. This way of dealing with the dilemma seems to be used with Dalit and non-Dalit members alike.

The other way in which pastors deal with this dilemma is an urban variant of "moving with the people." It involves not only being a friend to the Dalit members and identifying with them, but even giving them extra personal stroking, moral support and public recognition so that they feel equal to others. Some pastors have found that by openly identifying themselves as Dalits in personal conversations and group discussions, they have helped other Dalits do the same. One pastor said that because Dalit Christians often do seek the fellowship of other Dalit Christians but don't want this generally known, they go through him to find it. Another thought that it would be possible to form a cell of Dalit Christians in his pastorate for the purpose of carrying out a specialized ministry for Dalits.

There was no consensus at all among the pastors on how they or the

Church at large have helped Dalit Christians become more truly what God intends them to be through this kind of ministry. Some spoke in terms of such concrete help as finding educational and employment opportunities, others in terms of enhanced self-esteem, and yet others in terms of Dalits taking a larger role in the leadership of the church and giving more to it. One said that his congregation has grown a lot in size, three said that this kind of ministry had created greater unity, and another said that in his congregation it had increased Dalit political awareness and participation in the common Dalit struggle for justice, equality and dignity.

Yet, despite these gains, the urban pastors also had to report that casteism remains in the Church as a silent, subtle but powerful force. So too does a popular theology which fosters both insensitivity to the Dalits' plight and a willingness to accept passively the suffering casteism inflicts upon Dalits. Except for those industrial and railway workers who belong to labor unions, Dalit Christians normally remain silent about their Dalit identity and so are not in unity and solidarity either with each other or with other Dalits. Unemployment remains a serious problem, especially since Dalits cannot afford the donations demanded for seats in colleges and the bribes expected for middle class jobs in particular. Of special significance to several pastors is the fact that both the Church at large and individual pastors are so busy that the ministry to Dalits does not get the time, attention and energy which it deserves. They reported that in recent years many Dalit Christians have used their Church of South India congregations simply for holy communion, important Christian festivals, and family rites of passage, but turn to the Pentecostals for emotional worship, recognition, and a simple "feel good" theological message which helps them through the week. In short, there is much still to be done and some of that is within the Church's and even the individual pastor's power to change.

The urban pastors in the Punjab face a situation which resembles that of the rural rather than the urban pastor in and around Madras. The urban Punjabi congregations are not only almost totally Dalit but also relatively uneducated and poor. The pastors themselves must deal with the attitudes, expectations and behavior of a dependant and demoralized people and are perplexed about how best to do that. As one pastor put it, "it is very difficult to motivate them. They need everything without doing anything." Their reports also suggest that Punjabi Christians are more willing to be open about their Dalit origins than are those in and around Madras. Given this kind of pastoral situation, their patterns of ministry emphasizing education, guidance and problem-solving resemble those of the rural rather than the urban pastor in the Madras sample. The results of this kind of urban ministry are unclear.

No clear image of the urban pastor emerged from the consultation. Even though the facts of geography allow the urban pastor to have more frequent and intense contact with parishioners than is possible for the rural pastors, they are not the "head of the family" in the city as they are in the village congregation. The urban pastor is not the only educated middle class member of the parish; she or he is not the only innovator or problem solver for a congregation which has many alternative resources to draw upon. Urban pastors see themselves as working along side a few or many knowledgeable lay people of independent judgment, both Dalit and non-Dalit. Thus whereas the rural pastor may try to transfer power and responsibility to the lay leadership, in the urban parish power and responsibility are already in the hands of the laity. The urban pastor therefore tries to help guide their decision-making into the most fruitful channels for upbuilding the Church. Since ministry is shared with lay leaders who have "a variety of gifts," and since important decisions are taken after considerable consultation, the pastor is less free to "lead" and/or innovate, and pastoral ministry is more focused on "the religious" (broadly defined), which is the pastor's acknowledged specialty, than on the more generalized problem-solving which consumes so much of the rural pastor's time and energy.

CONCLUSIONS

This chapter has described the perceptions pastors have of ministry to Dalits. It has provided information on how they "read" their congregations and Dalit parishioners within the wider context of rural or urban life, how they have sought to minister to Dalit parishioners in the light of that reading, and what they thought the consequences were. The rural pastors see their Dalit people trapped in an environment in which there are few opportunities either to improve the quality of their lives or to escape to another, more promising environment. The urban pastors concentrate on the external circumstances of their parishioners' lives too, but see how their people's hiding a Dalit identity also prevents their becoming all that God has intended them to be. In the process of carrying out their pastoral responsibilities, the rural pastors can address their people's needs openly and directly (even if inadequately), whereas the urban pastors find that they must be more personal, indirect and private in their approach. This is because the urban pastors' congregations are more diverse and the pastors themselves must function within a framework of collective rather than individual leadership.

In their setting, as described in the previous chapter, the pastors are approached and move among the people as a patron among Dalit clients. The pastor comes to that role by calling and education rather than by right of birth and functions as a benevolent patron, there to serve Dalit clients so that they may no longer remain as clients in menial servitude but become instead heirs of the promises of God. The pastors' perceptions of ministry suggest that they have internalized the image of the pastor as "head of the family" moving among the people trying, by the grace of God, to solve their problems and lift their burdens. Like some of their missionary predecessors, they see their Dalit parishioners as "ignorant honest souls"[4] caught in a web of discrimination and oppression. Unlike the missionaries they see their parishioners more as people than as "work," more in secular than in religious categories. They also have a clearer vision of the political and socio-economic than of the psychological and spiritual aspects of their parishioners' lives.[5] The pastors express frustration more at their own inability to help than at their parishioners' mind-set or behavior patterns. Urban pastors share much of the outlook of the rural pastor but function in a setting where they can be at best only "modified patrons" and where their own Dalit background becomes problematic. Both urban and rural pastors speak with less confidence about Dalit women than about "generic" Dalit Christians. One Batala pastor may have summed this matter up rightly when he said that pastoring women hardly exists at all; "even if women are there, then still the [worship] service is not focused on them." All of the pastors were silent about

---

4 On this point the Batala pastors differ quite sharply from the Madras pastors.

5 Although this generalization is drawn from answers to specific questions asked in discussions as well as in the interview schedule and parish information form, the pastors were still given ample freedom to "frame" their pastoral situations in their own terms. I see this contrast as due to the influence primarily of liberation theology.

the deep inner struggles of the Dalit life, whether their own or that of others. This they may consider inappropriate to share.

In short, the pastors represent a subtly but profoundly indigenous style of ministry, seemingly congenial to pastor and Dalit parishioners alike. However, Christian theology has played only a minor role in articulating the perceptions upon which these conclusions are based. It is in the pastors' preaching that these perceptions interact with others drawn from Biblical and theological sources to provide theological vision and good news for the Dalits in the congregation.

CHAPTER 4

PREACHING THE GOSPEL

Preaching is an important, explicitly Christian, public act of ministry. It is also an act of ministry which can be examined fairly directly by reading sermons actually preached to congregations. In preaching the pastor brings his/her own perceptions of the people in a particular pastoral situation into relationship with the witness of scripture and Christian tradition, as the pastor perceives them, so as to convey the gospel to those people. Moreover, the sermon, unlike the liturgy, is not a "fixed form" of Christian communication. Instead, the preacher has great freedom to connect the Biblical witness to the lives of parishioners in a variety of ways. Consequently, the analysis of sermons provides valuable data for understanding how pastoral ministry to Dalits is actually being carried out.

Each of the pastors in the Madras group was asked to provide their most recent Christmas sermon, their most recent Easter sermon, and one other recent sermon of their own choosing for analysis. The Christmas and Easter sermons give insight into the pastors' presentation of the gospel at key moments in the Christian year, while the other sermons provide balance and some indication of common preaching patterns. Most of the fifty-one sermons were preached in Tamil and later translated into English by the preachers for analysis here; some also were clearly sermon summaries rather than full sermons. Nevertheless, they probably provide a reasonably accurate sample of the preaching which Dalit Christians in and around Madras hear on Sunday mornings. The analysis begins by describing the self-presentation of the preacher which may be inferred from certain common characteristics shared by virtually all of these sermons. Then the Christmas, Easter, and other sermons are examined in turn to see how they connect Christian theology with Dalit life.

THE SELF-PRESENTATION OF THE PREACHER

Preachers may have very clear, conscious understandings of who they are and what they are trying to do in and through their sermons. However, they may present, quite unconsciously, surprisingly different self-understandings through the style, structure and actual content of their sermons. What, then, is the functioning self-understanding, or self-presentation, of these preachers implicit in the their prevailing patterns of preaching? The answer to that question presented here is based upon such data as the use of Biblical material, the flow of argument, the nature and use of illustrations, and the kinds of appeals made to the congregation found in these sermons. The analytical focus will be, of necessity, less on the distinctiveness of individual sermons or preachers than upon shared characteristics of the sermons taken together. Five elements of a common self-presentation emerge from these 51 sermons.

1. *The preacher to Dalits is first and foremost a teacher.* The preachers describe and explain, addressing words primarily to the intellect and understanding. They make little or no direct appeal to intuition, emotion or imagination. They talk mostly about things "out there" or "back then," the truth of which is external both to the preachers and to the congregations. While a few sermons are characterized more by proclamation than by teaching, and while virtually all include some moral exhortation, the teaching mode is clearly predominant. This is true of Christmas and Easter sermons, of sermons preached in both urban and rural contexts, to both poor and middle class congregations.

Moreover, in teaching through preaching, the pastors seem to assume that the congregation will listen to their message passively and respectfully, with a basic openness and receptivity. The sermons do not provide evidence that the preachers are contending with parishioners who are actively engaging, and even challenging in their own minds, the preached word with the personal agendas, "conventional wisdom," nostalgia, or inner turmoil they bring to worship every Sunday. In short, the pedagogy of preaching appears to be the time-honored one that assumes a pupil's mind is a blank slate (tabula rasa) on which the teacher writes at will the message which the pupil is to learn.

2. *Specifically, the preacher is a teacher of Christian theology.* Preachers convey revealed truth about the human situation as well as about God's actions, nature, intentions, preferences, ways of relating to and dealing with human beings. Despite theological differences among them, preachers use theological affirmations above all to provide perspective in the light of which the members of the congregation are to see and live life. One preacher was very explicit about this in an

Easter sermon. "When we meet the Risen Lord," he said, "we get a new perspective, a new direction, in our life." He then went on to elaborate on how that worked. A few preachers referred to principles and lessons, but theological perspective is the main thing which these sermons provided.

3. *For the preacher the Bible is, almost exclusively, the sole source of theological truth.* Church tradition is totally ignored and the experience of the congregation is not used as a source of revelation. Reason is used to explain Biblically derived truth by analogy rather than as an independent source of truth. Moreover, most sermons stay within the Bible, using only Biblical illustrations and Biblical quotations as supporting evidence for the theological points being made. A few sermons never move out of the Bible at all. This can give the sermons an "other-worldly," or at least "different-worldly" aura.

4. *For the preacher the important thing is that the Biblical witness be heard, its perspective understood, and then applied.* In general, the preachers move, after a brief introduction, from the text of the Biblical witness, to its theological meaning and the perspective it therefore provides, to a closing application and exhortation. This source-explication-application pattern is usually repeated within each of the (generally three) points of the sermon, but in some cases it constitutes the three points of the entire sermon itself. For example, in a very simple and direct Christmas sermon, a rural pastor began with the text (source) "His name shall be called Emmanuel" (Matthew 1:23), explained with suitable Biblical illustrations that "Jesus brought God down to us. . . . Through Jesus we experience God's presence" (explication), and applied it by indicating (again, with appropriate Biblical examples) that the "us" God is with in Jesus are the poor, oppressed and powerless. As with many sermons, the application is left broad and general.

5. *The preacher, while referring to Dalits and Dalit experience, tends to keep them at a distance.* Dalits are almost always referred to in the third person ("them") rather than in the first person ("us"). They are talked about in a generalized way, simply as an abstract category of people, without names, faces, thoughts, feelings, dilemmas, flesh or blood. The preachers, with one possible exception, present only the exterior side of being a Dalit, i.e., a victim of external forces and circumstances. The preacher does not explore or reveal what being a Dalit feels likes or does to a person deep inside. Moreover, the Dalit

situation is treated completely ahistorically, as if it had remained completely static over the past one hundred years with neither a Christian movement nor a Dalit movement among them so far. Dalit liberation is located exclusively in the future; it is not depicted as a process which has already begun and is currently in progress. Sometimes one is given the impression that the sermon itself marks the inauguration of Dalit liberation in the region where it is being preached!

This fifth element of the preacher's self-presentation is perhaps the most surprising of all, since almost all of the preachers are themselves Dalits. Yet it is in keeping with the way almost all of contemporary human experience is treated. Aside from a lengthy poem in one sermon, the inner world of today's Christian or Indian people is not seen up close and is rarely referred to. This preference for distance over intimacy in preaching is difficult to explain. It may be part of the preacher's self-image as a detached professional or as one set apart. It could be a cultural or psychological preference, possibly as a function of an unstated or unconscious but nonetheless real patron-client relationship between preacher and congregation. Alternatively, the preachers may simply be following, quite unconsciously, the academic model of preaching used by their professors week after week in seminary chapel services. This matter clearly needs further exploration.

Since these five general characteristics are shared by all of the sermons, the analysis of Christmas, Easter and other sermons will follow the same pattern in turn. Each analysis begins by examining the movement the preachers make from their Biblical texts to their theological affirmations, then their movement from either their Biblical text or their theological affirmation to the Dalit situation, and finally what it is in the Dalit psychology which the preacher assumes makes the message preached good news to Dalits. That final step of analysis can be taken only by the use of inference because the sermons lack direct descriptions of or references to Dalit psychology.

THE CHRISTMAS SERMONS

Nine of the seventeen Christmas sermons analyzed are based upon Luke 2:1-20, or a portion thereof, as the guiding (as opposed to simply supplementary or supporting) text. The other traditional Christmas texts used were John 1:1-14 (twice), Luke 1:51-52, Philippians 2:5-11, and Isaiah 9:1-77. Three preachers selected quite different texts to present the Christmas message: John 10:10 (:"I am come that they may have life and have it more abundantly"); the story of Abraham, Sarah, and the birth of Isaac; and the parable of the Good Samaritan "which has the incarnation event hidden in it."

While two sermons place their text (John 1 and Luke 2) within the theological context of setting right the relationship between God and a fallen humanity, the others begin with the texts themselves and highlight their theological dimensions. This is done in one of two ways. One is to take certain theological statements within the texts themselves and elaborate upon them. For example, one preacher lifted up three verses of Luke 2 and explored the theological meaning of each: the glad tidings of great joy to all the people; it is tidings of peace and good will to all the people; it concerns a baby born in a manger. Another took the names (Wonderful, Counsellor, Prince of Peace) used in Isaiah 9 for the child to be born and elaborates on each. A third presented as good news the revolutionary impact the words of the Magnificat in Luke 1:51-52 have upon the moral, political, social and economic structures of society.

However, for most of the preachers it is the message contained within the Biblical text in conjunction with some special details of the historical context in which the message is given that provides theological significance. Thus, for example, what is theologically important is not just that God became a human being, but that this human being was born of refugee parents, in a dirty stable, in circumstances of poverty; that ordinary shepherds were made the first witnesses of his birth and he then grew up in a backward area like Galilee. Presumably, had Jesus been born among the rich and famous (like Gautama Buddha) the news would have been bad, or at least less good, because that would have distanced Jesus from most people.

The good news of Christmas is that God is with us, God identifies with us, God is reaching out to us, and drawing near to us; in Jesus God becomes accessible and approachable to us. God makes a new beginning in an old world, offers us abundant life, becomes one with us in order to liberate us. To quote one sermon,

to meet the powerless, he became powerless

to know the problems of the oppressed, he became oppressed

to identify with the problem of lower caste people, he identified himself as low caste.

In explaining why the angel's announcement of the birth of Jesus was good news to the shepherds, another preacher said:

It is good news to them that their light has come and that they will no longer be living in darkness, in ignorance. It is good news to them that their savior, the one who is going to bring peace on earth and good will among fellow human beings, has come. It is good news to them that God has decided and descended to be with them, among them and in them always.

What makes this good news to Dalits is the clear connection the preachers make between Jesus' poor parents, the shepherds, the ordinary Galilean people among whom he grew up, and today's Dalits. In coming to such people back then as God did, God comes also to Dalits today, for the similarities between the two peoples are so great as to make them virtually one. The similarities which are specifically mentioned most frequently are poverty, oppression, and being of no standing in society. Jesus was born among the world's victims, not among the victimizers, among the sinned against rather than the sinning. That is good news for the Dalits and bad news for the power elite (Herod, the priests, scribes, Pharisees, and their modern counterparts) whose privileged position has now been placed in jeopardy by Jesus' identification with the poor and outcaste.

Two psychological assumptions about Dalits seem to undergird this declaration of good news. The first is that Dalit Christians, like the preacher, see the world as divided between the haves and have-nots, that there is a perpetual conflict between these two categories of people, and that the Dalit Christians are clearly in the have-not category. The other assumption about Dalits is that they have deep within them a strong need to know or be reassured that God is indeed with them, that God does identify with them, and that God does reach out to them, is approachable and accessible to them. Although they do not mention it, perhaps the preachers assume that Dalits still feel polluted, unclean, and impure; that Dalits feel they are by nature unacceptable to God, in addition to feeling either socially or inherently inferior to others. Because this need and desire for divine affirmation is so deep within them, perhaps they take special delight in the fact that God has chosen to come in person first among their kind of people instead of among the rich and powerful.

THE EASTER SERMONS

The Easter sermons are based upon the resurrection narratives given in the four gospels and I Corinthians 15, with the lengthier accounts in Luke and John providing the preferred texts. What is particularly striking in the treatment of those texts is that the sermons focus attention far less upon what the resurrection did to Jesus than upon what it did to the disciples. Only two sermons make Jesus' transformation or the cosmic significance of his resurrection the major themes of the sermon and one other makes reference to that. All the rest simply proclaim the resurrection and then concentrate upon the changes which it brought about in the disciples. The transformations specifically referred to are almost exclusively psychological in nature (e.g., from fear to courage, sorrow to joy, self-centeredness to sacrificial love, hopelessness to new hope, new energy and new power). While much is made of the new mission Christ gives (mission being part of the transformation of the disciples), no mention is made of Christ opening up the way to heaven. One sermon focuses exclusively upon mission by posing and answering the question, "where do we find Christ today?". Another holds up the devotion of the women at Easter as a model for Christian devotion today.

In a small minority of Easter sermons, therefore, the movement is from the Biblical text to such theological affirmations as the risen Christ has power over death, the risen Lord is present among us, Christ is no longer bound by space and time, Christ has demonstrated the mighty power of God in his victory over evil and death, Christ is the living reality now and everywhere, the risen Christ empowers us to carry on his mission, the Holy Spirit is now present to help us and to intercede for us. For the vast majority of preachers, however, the good news of Easter lies primarily in God's, or Christ's, demonstrated power to transform individual lives, as exemplified by what happened to Jesus' followers on Easter and the days following it. One preacher took that a step farther by stating that the resurrection brought a peace which establishes justice and human rights, even for the weak and timid, as that is the kind of shalom Jesus gives.

Several sermons mention the events of Easter revealing, as did the events of Christmas, God's preference for the weaker sections of society. The evidence for this preference is provided by the women at the tomb and the angel's instructions, in Mark's and Matthew's gospels, to the disciples to return to Galilee to receive further instructions. Jesus' resurrection appearances to the women, which make them the first witnesses to the resurrection, are used in the same way as are the angel's appearance to the shepherds and God's choice of a poor marginalized couple to be the parents of God's son, namely to affirm, to elevate, and to give preference to the weaker sections of society. "In Christ there is a new status for the ladies and for the neglected people. The resurrection of Jesus Christ elevates the people who are not considered as equals." But there is a difference between Christmas and Easter. The women were not chosen simply for theological reasons; they were the ones who, of their own volition, went to the tomb early Easter morning. As one of these preachers said, among Jesus' followers "women are having more interest to see Jesus" and so went first to the tomb. This suggests that Jesus appeared to them first not because they were marginalized in Jewish (or Christian) society, but because they were the first among his followers to show up at the tomb and require an explanation for the fact that it was empty! Their devotion, not their status, made them the first witnesses.

The angel's message to the disciples through the women, recorded by Matthew and Mark, that the disciples would see Jesus in Galilee is used in the same ways as are the initial resurrection appearances to the women, namely to demonstrate God's preference for the weaker sections. "Jesus chose in poor and neglected Galilee to proclaim the news of the resurrection." "The risen Lord . . . is with the poor, depressed and outcastes." Yet this use of Matthew and Mark completely ignores Jesus' contradictory instructions to his disciples in Luke 24:49 to remain in Jerusalem until they are "clothed with power from on high," as well as the entire book of Acts which says that the Christian mission began in Jerusalem. This contradiction is not dealt with.

Those preachers who see in the events of Easter God's preference for the weaker sections of society connect the women at the tomb and Galilean priority to the Dalits. Dalits today are now in the same relative position that the women and Galileans occupied back then. However, the more common connection between the past event and the present is made by the resurrection itself. Christ is alive, and that provides living continuity between then and now. Thus, today's Dalits along with other believers, have access to the same transforming power of Jesus as did his original followers; Dalits too, whether they realize it or not, live in a world in which Christ has overcome the power of death and evil; and it is among them, and others like them, that the living Christ is to be found today, calling them to participate as his witnesses in his world-transforming mission.

What do the preachers assume to be present in the Dalit psyche which would make Easter good news to them? The majority of preachers seem to assume that Dalits long for personal transformation of the kind Jesus' early followers experienced: lives of hope, courage, joy, power, and meaningful participation in God's ongoing saving work. Presumably therefore, Dalits are not happy or satisfied with themselves as they are; they wish to be different kinds of people. If they were, their lives would be better than they are now. The minority of preachers, while not necessarily disagreeing, would lay their emphasis elsewhere. They see Dalits yearning for a new world in which not only is the law of karma broken but so also are the powers of this world as well as the forces of evil and death which hold Dalits captive. They want God's gift of personal and social well-being (shalom) most of all because they experience so little of it in their day-to-day lives.

THE OTHER SERMONS

The remaining eighteen sermons, when taken together, are quite diverse. They include sermons on such topics as prayer, faith, being prepared, participation in liberation, the Lord of history, the unity of the Church, and the diocesan mission themes. Some were prepared for such special days as Youth Sunday, Mission Festival, and Palm Sunday. Others were meditations on specific texts: Psalm 23, John 14:6, I Corinthians 1:18-25. Yet, despite this variety, the structure and wording of these sermons indicate that they fall into one of two categories. Most (15) are teaching sermons, setting forth a teaching and urging the congregation to follow it. These were what might be called "insider" sermons. They take Christian faith and life for granted, explain a part of it more fully, and then urge congregants to follow it more completely. Three sermons were "gospel" sermons which present the gospel message so that the congregation will receive it and trust it. These sermons have good news built into them. They do not presume "insider" status but recognize that there are those present who need to be drawn more fully inside.

The teaching sermons used as their basis either specific sayings in the text or specific people portrayed in the text. The words of Jesus, "love your neighbor as yourself," the verses of Psalm 23, Jesus' high priestly prayer in John 17, or his teaching on prayer in the Sermon on the Mount are set forth, explained and then the appeal is made to follow them. Alternatively, the examples of Jesus, or the Centurion, or the wise and foolish virgins are held up as models of behavior which the congregation is then urged to follow (or avoid). The psychological assumption underlying these sermons appears to be that if the congregation knows either what is right or what the ways of God are, and is then urged (perhaps with sufficient passion and conviction) to act accordingly, they will do so. In short, what the congregation really needs is enlightenment.

All three "gospel" sermons are based on John's gospel. While not excluding a didactic element, they appear to operate on different, or at least more varied, psychological premises. This can best be illustrated by referring to the sermons themselves. The entire emphasis of the first one, based on John 14:6, is upon life with Jesus who embodied the way and the truth and the life. "In the last analysis what man is always seeking is that which will make his life worth living. Life with Jesus is life worth living; it is life indeed." This sermon is full of phrases which suggest what makes life with Jesus worth living: Christ's companionship on the way, life with meaning and purpose no matter what our joys and sorrows may be, "freedom from anxiety over what is reality and what is illusion," freedom from doubt as to who we are (children of God and heirs of life), freedom to accept life as a challenge, life as a fresh chance.

A second sermon on "Life" invites the congregation to look at two Biblical examples of people who had received life through Jesus Christ. One was a case of "life threatened and safeguarded," the other of "life impaired and restored." The third sermon highlights selected verses about Jesus as the good shepherd. "I know my own and my own know me." [The gatekeeper] calls his own sheep by name. "The good shepherd lays down his life for the sheep." "There shall be one shepherd and one fold." All of these are suggestive and inviting phrases, aimed not just at the intellect and the will, but at the deeper yearnings of the human soul. These preachers seem to assume that one must touch more than the intellect in order to move people, whether Dalit or not, more fully inside the circle of faith, hope, and life.

Teaching sermons provide Dalits with enlightenment and guidance.

The assumption appears to be that Dalits want and seek these things. Perhaps it is an inner restlessness and discontent which drives them to break the shackles of ignorance, complacency and resignation which tie them down, and seek the transcendent wisdom which a Christian theological perspective can provide. "Gospel" sermons reach out to those Dalits who may have serious doubts about whether their lives are worth living, Dalits who have perhaps been so conditioned by the callous indifference or harsh contempt with which others treat them that they yearn for divine companionship and personal knowing, for meaning and clarity, for new beginnings, for the assurance of deep abiding love and genuine community.

CONCLUSIONS

In his book, *The Twice Alienated: Culture of Dalit Christians,* [1] the Osmania University philosopher, K. Wilson, presented a devastating critique of "salvation theology" as promoting psychological dependence, political passivity, and communal exclusiveness among Dalit Christians. The sermons analyzed here do not fall into that trap. Instead, the recurring message is one of divine affirmation of Dalits in general and God's empowerment of Dalit believers in particular for God's ongoing work of personal and social transformation in Jesus Christ. If one were to criticize these sermons in the light of what has been said in previous chapters, it would not be either for preaching a message that is in actuality bad news for Dalits or for seriously misreading their situation, but for a persistent mode of preaching which does not tap the full potential of the very good news for Dalits which the preacher has to share. Psychological assumptions about Dalits remain implicit and largely hidden, instead of being made explicit and addressed directly. The inner experience of Dalits, including the pastor's personal experience, is neither utilized as a preaching resource nor addressed in ways that give meaning and direction to the day-to-day struggles of Dalits.

When the pastors' sermons analyzed in this chapter are compared with their perceptions of pastoral ministry to Dalits presented in the previous chapter, a gap, or at least a tension, between the roles of pastor and

---

[1] (Hyderabad, 1982). For a brief analysis of this book and of Wilson's contribution to the development of Dalit theology, see John C.B. Webster,*The Dalit Christians: A History*, 234-236.

preacher appears. J. Randall Nichols has used these words to describe part of the dilemma.

We struggle with the roles of pastor and preacher, which do not fit easily together nearly as often as we would like to think. The pastor is a tolerant listener, committed to meeting people "where they are" and serving them by presence and shared experience. The preacher, by contrast, is a talker, a representative of the imperatives of the gospel and its claim on human life, an advocate for change and self-transcendence. How can one person consistently do both? We struggle with the human needs we are called to serve, trying to meet them in our pastoral work but then realizing in our proclamatory roles that often the gospel *defines* and *challenges* needs rather than meeting them. What do we do when the hopes and efforts of people who come to us for help are misdirected, as Christian faith would see it, yet in the agony of the moment no humane way of addressing that divergence appears?[2]

For the pastor/preacher to Dalits this dilemma is a serious one. How does the pastor/preacher relate the gospel of Jesus Christ to the many problems which rural Dalit parishioners bring to get "solved"? How can that message help change the outward circumstances of Dalit lives? How does the good news help urban Dalit Christians with their identity problems? Should the preacher, and how can the preacher, engage in the same kind of efforts, within a Christian theological and ethical framework, to undo the effects of social conditioning as the Chamars in Lucknow described earlier by Khare?[3] All of these questions beg the issue of what might be called "strategic pastoral preaching," i.e., allowing pastoral concerns to shape both the style and the content of preaching so that Dalit parishioners may be helped with what the pastor knows to be some of the deeper, more troublesome, and perplexing aspects of their lives. Strategic pastoral preaching which engages the stress and conflict of Dalit lives directly may prove to have greater healing and enabling power than does lectionary preaching in the present mode. On the other hand, such direct engagement may require important changes in the preacher's self-presentation and homiletical style. There are risks involved.

---

[2] J. Randall Nichols, *The Restoring Word: Preaching as Pastoral Communication* (San Francisco, 1987), 2.

[3] *Infra.*, 38.

CHAPTER 5

DALIT PARISHIONERS' PERCEPTIONS

Up to this point, pastoral ministry to Dalits has been examined almost exclusively through the perceptions of others. First, there were the missionaries whose records and accounts make up most of the available historical record. Next were the social scientists whose studies provide analyses of both the recent history and the wider Dalit setting of pastoral ministry to Dalits. The last two chapters presented the pastors' perceptions and from them inferences were also drawn about the pastors who did the perceiving. In order to round out the picture, this chapter is devoted to the perceptions of the Dalit parishioners themselves. These were gathered through a questionnaire which included both multiple choice and open-ended questions.[1] These questionnaire responses were supplemented by the author's notes on group discussions with Dalit parishioners in seventeen parishes in the Madras sample. They were then compared for points of contrast with the questionnaire answers of the Madras pastors themselves as well as with the Batala pastors' perceptions of how their parishioners might have answered some of the same questions. The Dalit parishioners' perceptions are intended to serve as a "reality check" on the perceptions of others, confirming some, challenging or contradicting others. The questionnaire deals with both the parishioners' inner world of outlook, disposition, identity and belief as well as their outer world of relationships, the church, and leadership. The data provided here, taken in conjunction with that in the previous chapters, provide the basis upon which the new pastoral priorities set forth in the concluding chapter were developed.

Each of the Madras pastors was asked to administer this questionnaire to a representative sample of ten Dalit members of the same parish within their pastorate described in their parish information forms. They were instructed to include least three women and three men as well as at least one person from each age group in the sample. In addition, the pastors were asked to make the sample representative of the education

---

[1] This questionnaire, together with the total number of responses given to each question (in parentheses) is found in Appendix E.

and occupations of Dalit members of the parish. Since one newly appointed urban pastor did not yet know who the Dalit members of his congregation were and another could get only five to be respondents, the total sample came to 175 respondents.

TABLE 2
OCCUPATIONS OF THE RESPONDENTS

Occupation	Total	Rural	Urban
Housewife	7	5	2
Unskilled daily wage laborer	27	23	4
Farmer,[2] crafts, or small business (rural)	14	13	1
Skilled labor	15	4	11
Teacher	27	5	22
Office Worker	18	4	14
Professional/ Officer in government or business	16	1	15
Rural Church worker[3]	10	10	0
Retired	22	7	15
Student/Unemployed	14	6	8
Other	4	1	3

The sample turned out to be very diverse indeed. There were 102 men and 73 women spread quite evenly over the age categories, with only the over 60 category being somewhat under-represented. Almost all were either first (24.6%), second (28.6%), or third (35.4%) generation Christians. Eighty of the respondents were from rural parishes and the remaining 95 were from urban parishes. Of the latter, 70 described theirs as a middle class congregation and 25 said that theirs was a poor

---

2 This probably refers to those who, unlike the daily wage laborers, either own land or are tenant farmers.

3 This category includes evangelists, Bible women, and village health guides employed by the diocese.

or working class congregation.[4] Thirty-six percent of the respondents described themselves as poor, 22.3% as "small people," 41.1% as middle class, and one as a "big person" within the Christian community.[5] Ten had no education at all; 17 had a primary and 30 had a middle school education. Fifty-eight were matriculates, 26 graduates, 27 post-graduates, and six had other (doctoral or professional) degrees. The occupations of the respondents are given in Table 2. Those in the retired category are almost as diverse as the sample as a whole, since they include former daily wage laborers and teachers as well as a retired foreign service officer and a high government official. Most of the unskilled laborers, rural farmers etc., and students or unemployed classified themselves as "poor." The occupational categories making up most of the "small people" were skilled labor, teachers, rural church workers and retirees. Teachers, office workers, professionals and officers provided most of the "middle class" sample. Such diversity in the sample increases confidence in the findings. However, despite the diversity in all of these important aspects of their lives, all the respondents belonged to the same jati, the Paraiyar or Adi Dravidas.

OUTLOOK AND DISPOSITION

The information presented in the previous chapters might lead one to expect Dalit Christians to be fatalistic and either depressed or angry people. However, their responses to a series of paired statements representing contrasting outlooks on life indicate that a significant majority of them (71.3% to 87.7%) believe that the world is basically a good place, that life is a wonderful gift, that things are going to get better for their families, and that their future has been and will continue to be largely in their own hands. There are few fatalists or pessimists among them. While this finding may appear surprising at first glance,

---

[4] Respondents from the same urban parish did not always agree on whether their particular parish was poor/working class or was middle class.

[5] These are categories which Lionel Caplan found were used by Protestants in Madras to describe themselves and others. Lionel Caplan, *Class and Culture in Urban India: Fundamentalism in a Christian Community* (Oxford, 1987), 11-14. The least well defined of these categories is the "small people." It is, however, both a cultural and an economic category. It is used here to provide a place for people who consider themselves neither poor nor middle class to locate themselves.

it is not inconsistent either with the Christian message they hear (as presented in the previous chapter) or with a recent analysis of general Dalit views.[6]

Who, then, are the dissenters? There is no one category of respondents which is in fundamental disagreement with the others. However, an outlook at odds with that of the vast majority, instead of being simply scattered at random throughout the entire sample, is sometimes found more frequently among some categories of respondents than among others. For example, a fatalistic outlook is found most frequently among the rural poor, but the majority of rural poor are not fatalistic. The answers to three questions all point in this direction. All eleven people who stated that their position in life today was due to their fate or karma belonged either to the rural poor or to the rural "small people." Similarly, fifteen of the 23 people who believed that being rich or poor is a matter of destiny one can do nothing about were rural poor, yet those fifteen constituted only 31% of the entire sample of rural poor. Thirty-six percent of those who said that health, happiness, disease and misfortune are all due to chance rather than human action were from the rural poor, but another thirty percent were from the urban middle class. On the other hand, on one question designed to test how people felt about life, the most significant dissent from a basically cheerful outlook came not from the rural poor but from women. While three-quarters of the respondents saw the world as a good place and life as a wonderful gift, only 18.6% of the men but 34.2% of the women considered the world evil and life a story of pain and suffering.

On one important question there was much less consensus. Just over half of the respondents indicated that the purpose of their lives was to be content and at peace, while just under one-third said that it was to make the world a better place for themselves and for others. Almost half of those who gave the first answer were poor; in fact, peace and contentment was the answer of about seventy percent of the poor. On the other hand, among those who chose making the world a better place were a larger percentage of men (36.3%) than of women (24.7%), of the middle class (44.4%) than of either the "small people" (33.3%) or the

---

6 These are based upon field work in rural Tamilnadu and a survey of the relevant scholarly literature on the subject. Lynn Vincentnathan, "Untouchable Concepts of Person and Society," *Contributions to Indian Sociology* 27 (January - June 1993), 54-82.

poor (15.9%), of those who have at least a bachelor's degree (40.7%) than of those with a middle school or secondary education (30.7%) or those with a primary education or no education at all (11.1%).

These findings on outlook are probably more reliable than the findings on disposition. People are generally more in touch with their conscious thoughts and attitudes than with the underlying psycho-dynamics of their lives. They may also be more willing to express their views than to bare their souls. These difficulties were borne in mind in framing the questions to probe such things as self-esteem, anger, shame, and inner longings; they must also affect any assessment of the answers given.

The majority of respondents described themselves as basically content (76%) rather than worried, anxious or frustrated; as persons with many strengths (63.2%) rather than many weaknesses; as capable of tolerating any situation of shame (73.1%); and as prepared to risk conflict in order to change things (73.7%). These answers would point to pervasive self-esteem and self-confidence; they would also challenge the view that Dalit Christians have a "wounded psyche." While those who are worried, anxious or frustrated appear more frequently in the rural (32.5%) than in the urban (16.8%) sample, they are not to be found in unusually large proportions among either the unmarried or the unemployed. Women are especially prominent among those who cannot bear shame. Forty-one percent of them, as opposed to only 16.7% of the men, described themselves in this way. Moreover, this response was far more frequent among poor (45.5%) and "small" (75%) women than among middle class (21.4%) women. Women (38.4%) also showed a more pronounced tendency than men (17.6%) to let things be as they are in the interests of peace and harmony. This was especially true of poor (48.5%) and "small" (41.7%) but not of middle class (25%) women.

The overwhelming majority of respondents (89.7%) described themselves as angry only some of the time, while another four percent said that they were almost never angry. What provoked the respondents' anger most readily were insults to their dignity or pride (31%), frustration or disappointment (18.4%), being lied to or cheated (15.5%), opposition (12.1%),[7] and injustice (15.5%). The most common

---

[7] Many respondents in this category referred specifically to disobedience by children, whether their own or those whom they teach in school.

expressions of anger were lashing out verbally (45.6%) or repression either by turning the anger inward or by walking away (40.1%). Only a few (7.6%) used prayer.

Fear of God's rejection was the most commonly expressed fear (43.7%) among the respondents. About half of the men expressed this as their fear, whereas only about one-third of the women did. The other most commonly cited fears (24.1%) fell into the category of "future events I cannot control." Fear of one's own weaknesses and mistakes was slightly more common among men (18.6%) than among women (11%). For just under a majority of the respondents family well-being was both their major prayer concern and the subject their minds most often wandered on to. Second in the latter category were their own personal lives, worries, hopes and problems.

These results are somewhat problematical. For one thing, the Batala pastors took issue with two major findings. They believed that their parishioners were more fatalistic than this survey would suggest. This difference the Batala pastors attributed to the higher level of education among Dalit Christians in the south. However, this survey did not find fatalism to be significantly more common among the less than among the better educated. Thus, if the Batala pastors' perception is accurate, there must be another reason for it. The Batala pastors also took issue with the finding concerning capacity to bear shame. One pastor summed up the consensus among the Batala group when he said that, "Whatever they [Punjabi Dalit Christians] may say, they cannot bear shame." It should also be noted that the survey findings concerning self-esteem and shame are at odds with the perceptions of the urban pastors reported in chapter three. Moreover, all the findings about disposition in particular contradict the main body of psychological research referred to in chapter two.

There are three possible explanations for these contradictions. The first, and probably the most obvious, is that there is a difference between the north and the south. As was noted earlier, the psychological research was based almost exclusively upon north Indian samples. Yet, if a difference in disposition between north and south Indian Dalits exists, there is no explanation for it so far. The second possible explanation of the contradiction has to do with the impact of conversion to Christianity. Christian faith could have in fact brought changes in the level of self-confidence and the Madras sample could be comprised of Dalits who have more fully internalized the gospel message than have their Punjabi counterparts. In other words, years of Christian worship, teaching and community may have borne some good psychological and spiritual fruit. This would also account for the difference between Christian Dalits in this sample and the other Dalits used for the psychological research cited in chapter two. The other explanation is that the pastors' perceptions are simply more accurate than are the responses to the questionnaire. Dalit Christians may wish to provide "more Christian" answers to the questionnaires than is warranted by the facts of their inner lives; they may have used the questionnaire to hide rather than to reveal their inner turmoil. In a discussion with some Dalit Christians at Arakkonam, it was the consensus of the group that "we are fifty percent healed." Although it lacks precision and specificity, this may be the best explanation of Christianity's impact yet. Clearly more and better research in this important area is required before less tentative conclusions can be arrived at.

IDENTITY

It was the Madras pastors' perception, pointed out in chapter three, that urban Dalit Christians struggle with and often try to hide their Dalit identity. The pastors considered such behavior to be indicative of inner shame and low self-esteem. As it happened, the survey questions on identity uncovered far more of this inner uncertainty and ambivalence than did the more direct questions on disposition. The identity questions were based on the assumption that Dalit Christians are more open and clear about their Christian than about their Dalit identity. This assumption proved to be correct not only for the urban but also for the rural Dalit Christians. Moreover, the answers to questions on Dalit identity revealed far more inner tension, and even contradiction, than did those on Christian identity.

"Christian" is the label generally used by 65.5% of the sample when describing themselves to other people. Another 11.4% used a more specific religious identity (Protestant, Church of South India) and 17.7% used a caste identity (Harijan, Scheduled Caste, Dalit), while only 5.1% used their occupation or job title instead. The preference for "Christian" was spread quite evenly throughout the sample, although the men seemed to use it somewhat more frequently than the women.[8]

---

[8] It was the choice of 71.8% of the men but of only 59.5% of the

When asked specifically whether they preferred being called a Christian or a Dalit Christian, 64.2% opted for the former and 35.8% for the latter label. However, "Dalit Christian" was preferred by half the respondents with post-graduate degrees, and was preferred more by first and second generation Christians (41.9%) than by those whose families had been Christians for longer than that (28%). Probably local circumstances and local custom play an important, if not deciding, role in determining which label one generally uses. All ten respondents in one parish and nine of the ten in another preferred "Dalit Christian;" on the other hand, in three parishes nobody and in four others only one respondent preferred it. In the former category was a rural parish and an urban parish which was overwhelmingly Dalit; in the latter were three rural (completely Dalit) parishes as well as three urban parishes in which Dalits were a minority.

A very large number of respondents (81.3%) indicated that they were proud to be Dalits.[9] Nonetheless disclosure of Dalit origins and identity proved to be a difficult issue. The sample was fairly evenly divided among those who felt that one must be cautious about this (36.1%), those who considered it a necessary risk for the sake of freedom (36.1%), and those who considered disclosure to be a matter of Christian conviction (27.8%). The answers concerning the pattern of disclosure are given in Table 3. As the table indicates, the patterns are fairly uniform for all three classes as well as among urban and rural people. For the majority at least a modified openness ("only when asked") seems to be the norm.

It is when comparing answers to the questions about disclosure that the tensions and ambivalence begin to appear. Of the 135 respondents who felt neither ashamed nor cursed to be a Dalit, forty felt that they had to be cautious about revealing their identity openly. Similarly, of the 108 respondents who felt one should be open either as a matter of Christian conviction or to experience freedom, six never disclose their caste identity, eleven do so only among relatives and close friends, and five do so only on matters related to the government's reservation policy. There are inconsistencies here which point to inner tensions and uncertainties. Only 79 or 45.1% of the entire sample of 175

___

women.

[9] Those who felt ashamed or cursed to be Dalits were most prominent among the rural poor (29.2%).

TABLE 3
WHEN DALIT CHRISTIANS DISCLOSE THEIR CASTE IDENTITY

Response	Total Sample	Rural	Urban	Poor	Small People	Middle Class
Never	8.6%	3.8%	12.6%	3.2%	7.7%	18.9%
Only among friends or members of my caste	17.1%	11.3%	22.1%	22.2%	20.5%	11.1%
Only on matters related to the governments' reservation policy	8.0%	13.8%	3.2%	11.1%	10.3%	4.2%
Only when asked	44.0%	48.8%	40.0%	41.3%	35.9%	50.0%
On all occasions	22.3%	22.5%	22.1%	22.2%	25.6%	20.8%

respondents were proud to be Dalits, believed openness was either desirable or necessary, and actually were at least moderately ("only when asked") open, if not completely open, in practice. This kind of consistent openness was found slightly more among urban (49.5%) than among rural (40%) respondents, and much more among middle class (58.3%) than among either poor (34.9%) or "small" (35.9%) respondents. This suggests that upward mobility does ease but does not eliminate the "identity problem" for Dalit Christians.

The findings concerning Christian identity are quite different. The reasons why respondents consider themselves Christians are given in Table 4. These findings indicate that the rural respondents seem to have a more communitarian outlook on being a Christian (emphasizing birth, being part of the community, and baptism), whereas the urban respondents have a more individualistic outlook (emphasizing personal faith and behavior). The middle class is also noticeably the most individualistic and the poor the most communitarian in outlook. When asked an open-ended question about why they remained Christians, virtually all gave answers expressing inner conviction: to be a witness (46.9%), for my own salvation (13.1%), to worship the true God (19.4%), Christ's teachings are best (8%), and to serve others in Christ's way (8.6%). Three women did mention having married into Christian families as their reason.

Some of the inner uncertainty and tension about Dalit identity which is apparent in the questionnaire also came out in group discussions with urban Dalit Christians. In one such discussion, the participants always referred to Dalit Christians as "they" or "them" rather than as "we" or "us." So did another one until a very prominent man in the group made a comment which indicated that he was a Dalit; that seemed to give permission for the others to do the same, with the result that the conversation became much more open, free and productive. In a third, one person made the observation (validated by the second conversation itself as well as by the pastoral experience referred to in chapter three) that "we can help each other if we are open." However, the most poignant was a heated discussion in a fourth urban parish provoked by a young man who said, "I degrade myself by telling I am a Dalit after attaining status equal to others." The pros and cons on this were argued strongly for some time. When I commented that the argument itself proves that Dalit Christians have special problems we need to think about, the young man replied, "I don't even like to think about it." It

TABLE 4
"WHY I AM A CHRISTIAN"

Response	Total Sample	Male	Female	Rural	Urban	Poor	Small People	Middle Class
I was born in a Christian Family	34.5%	35.3%	33.3%	41.3%	28.9%	44.4%	30.8%	28.4%
I belong to the Christian Community	7.3%	5.8%	9.3%	11.3%	4.1%	7.9%	10.3%	5.4%
I was baptized	10.7%	4.9%	18.7%	15.0%	7.2%	15.9%	10.3%	6.8%
I follow the teachings of Jesus	14.7%	18.6%	9.3%	11.3%	17.5%	9.5%	15.4%	18.9%
I have faith in God and Jesus	30.5%	33.3%	26.7%	18.8%	40.2%	20.6%	28.2%	39.2%
I attend church services regularly	1.1%	1.0%	1.3%	1.3%	1.0%	0.0%	2.6%	1.4%
I don't know	1.1%	1.0%	1.3%	1.3%	1.0%	1.6%	2.6%	0.0%

was simply too painful. In one rural parish it was observed, with obvious regret about having to mention caste, that "we are being open only to get government benefits."

It is this inner uncertainty, tension and inconsistency around Dalit identity issues which points to the deep wound in what could otherwise be a generally healthy, even robust, collective psyche. The Madras pastors were themselves almost totally consistent about being both unashamed and open. The Batala pastors pointed out that the common Punjabi word for Christian, "Isai," has a (Dalit) caste component built into it. They also disagreed with the Madras findings about why Dalit Christians remain Christians. The Batala group's perception was that Punjabi Dalit Christians really have nowhere else to go. They don't want to be Chuhras again as that is a step downwards; they probably wouldn't be accepted by other Chuhras who are reluctant to share their scheduled caste benefits; and Dalit Christians consider the Church to be a more reliable source of help than the government anyway. "We are Christians and that is that."

RELATIONSHIPS

It has been a major premise of government policy and of much popular thinking that with increased urbanization, modernization and "reserved" opportunities to move up in class status, untouchability would diminish and the social integration of "the weaker sections" would improve over time. Even though Dalit Christians are not eligible for many scheduled caste benefits,[10] the data gathered here provides some support for that premise and even some indication that progress is being made. Only 38.9% of the respondents said that untouchability was being practiced where they live and work. Among the rural poor, however, the percentage was 56.3%, while it was only 24.2% among the urban population as a whole. Where it exists, the practice of untouchability takes a variety of forms: the denial of housing or of entry into homes and shops, the refusal of food exchanges, avoidance of physical proximity, or discrimination in posting and promotion at work. Of these the rural poor mentioned the

---

[10] Only 30.3% of the sample had actually received any scheduled caste or backward class benefit from the government. Of these, urban Dalit Christians got most of the scholarships and jobs, while rural Dalit Christians got most of the development assistance.

first most frequently.

The responses to further questions provided additional evidence that the rural poor, the section of the population least affected by planned social change, remain the chief victims of untouchability and caste discrimination. Moreover, they consider themselves discriminated against because they are Dalits and not because they are Christians. When asked whether a distinction was made between Christian and other Dalits where untouchability was practiced, an almost equal number answered "yes" and "no."[11] The group which experienced such distinctions most frequently were urban middle class men (50% yes vs. 28.1% no), while the rural poor experienced them least (50% no vs. 29.2% yes).[12] More respondents (50) felt that being a Christian was a barrier to their advancement than felt being a Dalit was.[13] On the other hand, over three times as many respondents felt excluded from social groups and social occasions because they were Dalits (66) than because they were Christians (21). Five-eighths of all the rural poor respondents put themselves in the former category;[14] those in the latter category were spread throughout the sample. A slight majority (54.3%) considered their present job and income to be in accordance with their merits. Of those who did not, the poor (63.5%) and "small people" (53.8%) were far more prominent than the middle class (25%).

The Dalit Christian situation within the Christian community is different. For one thing, only 18.4% of the respondents reported that Christians where they live and work practice untouchability. That is less than half of those who reported it for society as a whole. However, another 10.9% did indicate that non-Dalit Christians discriminate against them in other ways. The other difference is that it is not the

---

11 The division was 34.3% yes, 35.4% no, and the remaining 30.3% either did not answer the question or did not consider it applicable.

12 The significance of this finding for the urban middle class is unclear because no follow-up question was asked to find out whether the Dalit Christian respondents felt they were treated better or worse than other Dalits were. Half the rural poor, however, felt that they were treated just the same as other Dalits were.

13 This is probably because Christian Dalits are denied the scheduled caste benefits granted to other Dalits.

14 This is a very high percentage considering the fact that 50.3% of the entire sample did not feel excluded at all!

rural poor but the urban middle class men who most frequently reported experiencing untouchability by other Christians. (Those who reported other forms of discrimination were spread evenly throughout the sample.) The evidence most frequently cited, especially by the urban middle class (37.5%) and "small" (47.1%) men, was that "no real fellowship is offered."[15] One spoke of a non-Dalit Christian ending a good friendship upon learning that the respondent was a Dalit; another referred to the "bye-bye" culture in the congregation. Other studies indicate that rural caste Christians do practice untouchability against rural Dalit Christians;[16] in this sample, however, there were no caste Christians in the villages inhabited by the respondents. This probably explains why untouchability among Christians shows up here only in the urban churches.

All of the group discussions in urban parishes indicated that caste was a real problem for the Dalit Christians. They differed only in their assessments of how serious the problem was and how best to deal with it. In a couple of parishes, where the Dalits comprise a good percentage of the membership, a direct, even confrontational approach was advocated. Most, however, preferred to be more cautious. Among them several have simply been silent, acknowledging that silence (and hence neglect) is the price they pay for unity. Others fear an inevitable backlash and even splits in the parishes if Dalit ministry issues are raised. One well-educated woman indicated that such an approach is really counter-productive. "The more you make it an issue, the more the backlash. If you relax, they get annoyed and let go of the issue. If you allow them to bug you, you're bugged forever!" One upper middle class group was of the opinion that their situation is not very bad and is likely to improve because the younger generation cares about caste even less than they do. "Well placed people just don't have the time or interest to bother about these things." Thus they were inclined to let nature take its course.

This view is too sanguine. The data reveals a significant degree of alienation among Dalit Christians. A 55.8% majority indicated that the high castes will always misuse the Dalits instead of seeing harmony

---

15 These percentages are unusually high since only 18.3% of the entire sample gave this response.

16 These studies are mentioned and summarized in John C.B. Webster, *The Dalit Christians: A History*, 179-182.

with the high castes as the path to Dalit well-being. This response was particularly noticeable (69%) among respondents under 30 years of age. Moreover, a similar majority (56%), from which the "small people' (38.5%) dissented, did not see Dalit Christians imitating the food habits and dowry system of the higher castes, thus suggesting that the latter are not necessarily considered models worth emulating. The respondents attribute the poor treatment which Dalits receive at the hands of other castes mostly to either caste prejudice (38.3%), or their own poverty (33.7%), or their lower level of education (11.4%). A majority (57.6%) of those for whom poverty was the cause are poor and poverty was the reason given by a majority of the poor (54%). In like manner, a majority of the middle class (51.4%) said caste prejudice was the cause, and a majority (55.2%) of those who attributed bad treatment to caste prejudice were middle class. When asked what the worst consequences of the caste system have been, the respondents gave an impressive list of social ills: social divisions and alienation (21.7%), social inequality, discrimination and oppression (32%), [17] degradation or psychological damage (26.3%), and communal violence (18.3%). These responses were spread quite evenly throughout the sample, except that the number of rural poor mentioning psychological damage was somewhat higher than average (35.4%).

Dalit Christians report no such alienation either from other Dalits or among themselves. Fifty-two percent indicated that, where they live and work, relations between Christian and non-Christian Dalits are either good or excellent, while another forty percent said they were satisfactory. The rural poor were the most positive (68.8%), while the urban middle class were much less so (31.6%).[18] Even though there was no consensus about the issues on which Christian and non-Christian Dalits should unite,[19] 90.9% believed that such a joining of

---

[17] Those 12 respondents who referred to bonded labor and slavery have been added to this category.

[18] These figures are the percentage of rural poor and urban middle class respondents respectively who indicated that relations were either good or excellent.

[19] The responses were: for political reasons/to obtain our rights (23.1%); for safety and security of life (22%); to get our basic needs met (17.9%); for respect and dignity (16.8%); to make social and economic progress (20.2%).

hands would indeed take place.[20] Again, there was no consensus about the reasons for this optimism, but the reasons given are realistic and pragmatic: such unity is already taking place and proving successful (14.5%); we share a common plight (21.1%); we are already neighbors (13.2%); it is in our interests to do so (10.5%); it is our best hope for a good life (27%); and "unity is strength" (13.8%). In like manner, the respondents considered fellowship with other Dalit Christians either important (54.9%) or very important (41.1%) to them. While more said that successful Dalit Christians never help (24) than usually help (12) their fellow Dalit Christians, most indicated that they do so about half the time (27.1%) or occasionally (51.8%).

At the end of this section of the questionnaire there were three questions about the image and "place" of women among Dalit Christians. When asked an open-ended question about the difference they saw between Christian and other Dalit women, only a small percentage (18.5%) saw little or no difference at all. The rest mentioned better habits and life-style (40.5%),[21] education (18.5%), a better religious life (10.4%), and such psychological differences as courage and confidence (12.1%). Indeed a 62.3% majority considered the contrast between Christian and non-Christian Dalit women to be greater than the contrast between Christian and non-Christian Dalit men. This would suggest that Christianity has had a greater impact upon the women than upon the men. When asked who controls the money within Dalit Christian families, almost exactly half the respondents indicated that both husband and wife share control of their combined incomes; the remaining half said that it was controlled by the husband alone (31.5%), or the wife alone (14%), or else he controlled his and she controlled hers (4.7%). On all three questions there were no noticeable differences in the responses of men and women, except that men (45.1%) were more apt to distinguish Dalit Christian women from other Dalit women by their better habits and life-style than were the women themselves (32.9%).

The Madras pastors were in general agreement with their parishioners. The percentage of pastors who found untouchability being practiced

---

20 Eight of the fifteen dissenters came from one urban parish. Most gave as their reason that Christians are a minority people.

21 Those five respondents who referred to hygiene have been included in this category.

among Christians was somewhat higher, as was the percentage expressing alienation from the higher castes. More also attributed maltreatment of Dalits to caste prejudice. On the other hand, fewer pastors than lay people were optimistic about the possibility of Christian and other Dalits joining together. On only one point did the pastors seriously disagree with their parishioners; a better than two-thirds majority found Dalit Christians imitating the dowry system and food habits of the higher castes. The Batala pastors also were in basic agreement with those survey findings on relationships which were made available to them.

The network of relationships with the higher castes, with Christians of other castes, with other Dalits, and with each other constitutes much of the context within which ministry to Dalit Christians takes place. This survey indicates not only that Dalit Christians do not share a single or unified perception of those relationships but also that their perceptions do not fall into neat, mutually exclusive compartments according to sex, class, age, education, urban or rural location. Instead their perceptions tend to blend into each other across a fairly wide spectrum of views. For example, the sharpest contrast running throughout the survey is between the perceptions of the rural poor and those of the urban middle class. Yet even their perceptions overlap at almost every point; the statistics merely indicate that certain responses are more frequent within some categories of age, class, sex, or location than within others. Moreover, while the evidence here does provide some general support for the view that modernization has reduced the practice of untouchability and led to increased integration of Dalits with the rest of Indian society, there is also enough evidence of division, alienation and conflict to suggest that modernization has failed in both respects. Thus the picture of the Dalit Christian situation which emerges is one of diversity, complexity and nuance to which those engaged in ministry must be sensitive.

BASIC BELIEFS AND THE CHURCH

This section of the questionnaire attempts to explore the religious consciousness, piety and spirituality of Dalit Christians by finding out what they consider important in their Christian faith and corporate congregational life, especially its worship. It adopts an inductive and operational rather than normative understanding of both basic Christian beliefs and the Church. It therefore asks questions about Dalit Christian perceptions of the relationship which Christ and the Church have to their lives rather than about the respondents' conformity to or deviation from an accepted inventory of Christian doctrines and practices. The results are rather chaotic. Dalit Christians exhibit a wide range of perceptions in such a variety of combinations as to make generalizations virtually impossible. There are few correlations not only between perceptions and social circumstances but also between one perception and another. Several of the correlations which do exist do not seem to "make sense." This suggests that the pastor may have to engage in ministry to Dalit Christians with sensitivity to rather than a clear understanding of this very important, even definitive, aspect of their lives.

The most important sources from which Dalit Christians have gained an understanding of what to believe and do as Christians are their parents (38.8%) and the Bible (43.8%). As it happened, poor women (51.5%) and third generation Christians (51.6%) were the ones who most frequently mentioned their parents as the primary source of such understanding. On the other hand, those with post-graduate degrees (54.5%), "small people" in general (56.4%), and first generation Christians (58.1%) most frequently mentioned the Bible as their primary source.[22] Surprisingly, few considered either Sunday worship (5.1%) or the pastor (0%) to be primary influences. This response begs the question of how the Bible exercises its influence; it could do so either directly on its own, or as it is "mediated" and interpreted by pastors and catechists in the context of worship and Christian education, or both. This needs further exploration.

The respondents' views of salvation were quite diverse with no one view generally predominant. "Forgiveness of my sins" was the most frequently mentioned (36%), followed by going to heaven (23.4%), liberation of the oppressed (21.1%), abundant life for believers here and now (15.4%), and a new heaven and a new earth (4%). However, going to heaven was the choice of 54.5% of the poor women (in contrast to only 26.7% of the poor men). Liberation of the oppressed was chosen by more of the rural men (39.1%) than of any other category of respondents. The other choices were spread quite evenly throughout the

---

[22] Why this particular combination of categories should be influenced more than others by the Bible is difficult to explain; it can only to noted here and left for the reader to ponder.

sample. A good majority (56.3%) believed that Jesus was a Dalit; another 20.1% were not sure. One respondent said that "this is absurd" and several pointed out that Jesus was God. The belief that Jesus was or was not a Dalit, like the use of the self-designation "Dalit Christian" referred to earlier, seems to be a matter of local usage. In six of the eighteen parishes surveyed, either eight or nine of the ten respondents said Jesus was a Dalit, while in four others only one or none said he was. In the remaining eight parishes the responses were quite mixed.

When asked open-ended questions both about how Christ helps them in their everyday life and about the gifts Christ gives to Dalit Christians, the answers were very diverse and revealed no clear patterns according to sex, class, urban and rural location. The kinds of help mentioned included friendship, knowledge and wisdom for my problems, protection, meeting my daily needs, and family advancement. The major categories were guidance (24.9%), support (22.5%), companionship (16.8%), problem-solver (13.3%), and bestower of benefits (22.5%). In like manner, the gifts Christ gives Dalit Christians include a new identity, status, peace, musical talent, capacity for hard work, ability to manage problems, courage and boldness, contentment, hospitality, a different life-style, and forgiveness. The major categories were material benefits (15.3%), spiritual gifts (31.8%), a new quality of life (21.8%), and the ability to deal with life's challenges (16.5%). A significant 78.2% majority said that Christ gives these gifts to other Dalits as well.

There was no discernable internal relationship among views of salvation, the kinds of help Christ gives for everyday life, and the gifts Christ gives Dalit Christians. Thus, for example, people who see salvation as going to heaven perceive Christ's help and gifts no differently than do those who see salvation as liberation of the oppressed. There is not even a relationship between the kinds of help and the kinds of gifts Christ gives! Perhaps the categories used to classify the answers were not the best. Clearly, further investigation is needed because this preliminary attempt has yielded little beyond unexplained diversity.

Most of the respondents (57.6%) attend church services in order to worship God. Some go to seek God's favor (14.1%), to learn more about their faith (13%), or because they consider it to be their Christian duty (9%). A 55.1% majority said that the sermon was the most important part of the service for them. Among the reasons given for this preference were that the sermon increases understanding of the Bible, helps us know the promises of God, teaches us how to live in the world, helps us grow in spiritual life, strengthens our relationship with God, and is interesting. Those 18.6% who considered the prayers most important said that prayers help me pour out my feelings, share burdens, and forget this world; prayers also purify the heart, bring victory and blessing, and create one family. Singing, preferred by 15.6% of the respondents, enables me to forget this world and its worries, express feelings, praise God, and attain ecstasy; singing also provides inspiration and attracts people of other religions. The Lord's Supper, the choice of 9.6%, provides fellowship with Jesus, a reminder of his suffering, honor to God and to other human beings; it is also an occasion of fellowship, of remembrance, and of grace in which sins are washed away. Four respondents indicated that worship does not help them in their daily lives and another fourteen did not know how it did. The kind of help it did provide for most, however, was spiritual and psychological (44.7%), guidance in leading a Christian life (33.5%), fellowship and community (11.2%). A slight majority (51.4%) said that "Sunday worship must change to include more participation of members" rather than remain as it is. Those most in favor of more participation were the graduates (65.4%) and post-graduates (75.8%).

Two questions were asked to find out what kinds of hopes the respondents had for their congregations. One was phrased in terms of what they thought God wanted the congregation to do in the next three years and the other in terms of the respondent's own "number one wish for this congregation." The two questions yielded similar results. Several parishes had plans for specific building projects (a new church building, repairs or an addition to the existing one, a new parsonage) and 7.9.% of the respondents believed God wanted the congregation to remain as it was. Most, however, spoke in general terms of evangelistic outreach, numerical growth, a better quality of spiritual life, greater Christian unity, and improved ministries of social justice and social service to the poor.[23] Here also there were no clear connections between basic beliefs and hopes for the church. For example, the proportion of those giving priority to ministries of social service and social justice, while small in both cases, was nonetheless twice as high among those who saw salvation as going to heaven

---

23 Similar kinds of hopes were expressed in the parish group discussions as well.

(17.1% & 22%) than among those who saw salvation as liberation of the oppressed (8.1% & 10.8%)!

The Madras pastors differed from their parishioners primarily in displaying a more homogenous religious consciousness. Over two-thirds saw salvation primarily as liberation of the oppressed; four-fifths experienced Christ's personal help as guidance; virtually all saw Christ giving either spiritual gifts or a new quality of life to Dalit Christians. The Batala pastors did not have a chance to respond to all of these questions, but on one there was emphatic disagreement. The most important part of the church service for their parishioners was the singing, not the sermon. One commented, "People leave when the pastor preaches!"

Taken together, all the evidence in this section indicates that Dalit Christians do not share a common religious consciousness, spirituality or piety. In fact, there are not even clear and distinct types of Dalit Christian religious consciousness, whether defined by social groupings (urban vs. rural, young vs. elderly, well educated vs. relatively uneducated, poor vs. middle class) or by specific theological orientations (liberal, conservative, liberationist, pietist, etc.). There is just too much diversity, complexity, and apparent randomness to fit the data into such categories. Moreover, these indicators of religious consciousness do not appear to be directly and deliberately linked up to the problems of disposition, identity, and relationships revealed in earlier sections of this chapter. Perhaps the questions were wrongly phrased or the answers wrongly classified; perhaps also the questions did not and could not probe deeply enough. On the other hand, this situation of unexplained diversity may be due to the fact that up to this time pastoral ministry to Dalit Christians has not really focused specifically upon them and upon the inner realities of their Dalit Christian lives. As a result, ministry to them may itself have had a random quality, lacking well conceived, intentional, long-term efforts to develop their religious consciousness, piety and spirituality in those ways that hold out the greatest promise of healing, wholeness and liberation in the contexts within which they live.

LEADERSHIP

It was the Madras pastors' perception that the pastor is the "head of the family" and problem-solver for the rural parish, whereas in the

urban parish leadership is shared and the pastor is a guide to collective decision-making. Three questions were designed specifically to discover the Dalit parishioners' preferred style of leadership. The first was an open-ended question concerning the expectations Dalit Christians had of their leaders. The other two were multiple choice questions concerning the most important characteristic of a Church leader and the kind of leader they think would be most helpful in their congregation. The assumption behind these and other questions concerning leadership was that, since the pastors were administering the questionnaires, indirect questions about leaders in general would yield more reliable results than would questions directly about pastoral leadership itself. The results are worth noting because they do provide insight not only into Dalit Christian assessments and preferences concerning leadership but also into those Dalit Christian problems and needs which may lie beneath the surface and account for their particular assessments and preferences.

For a plurality of almost forty percent of the respondents, the most important thing Dalit Christians expect of their leaders is "a person who helps us with our problems in practical ways." This response was especially frequent among the rural poor (54.2%) and was repeated in group discussions in rural parishes. This finding thus provides justification for the "problem-solver" image rural pastors have of themselves. The other common expectations Dalit Christians had of their leaders were a good Christian character (24.3%) and someone who treats them with love, care, patience and fairness (27.7%). These two responses were spread quite evenly throughout the sample. For almost a majority (46.6%), the most important characteristic of a good church leader was that he/she be "a wise and clear teacher and guide." The other two choices of preference were that they be spiritual persons, the choice of 24.3% of the sample as a whole but of 35.1% of the urban middle class respondents, and that they be "courageous champions of the people's interests" (24.4%). Views about the most helpful kind of leader for the congregation are also diverse.

The responses given in Table 5 do indicate some differences between men and women, between rural and urban people, and between the classes, three of which deserve special comment. The differences between men and women on making decisions according to established practice, and perhaps on encouraging the people's ideas, may reflect the relative absence of women in the pastorate's decision-making process.

TABLE 5
"THE MOST HELPFUL KIND OF LEADER IN THIS CONGREGATION"

Response	Total Sample	Male	Female	Rural	Urban	Poor	Small People	Middle Class
Gives clear, strong, direct guidance to the people	33.3%	30.4%	37.0%	38.8%	28.4%	36.5%	25.6%	33.3%
Gives encouragement and support to the peoples' ideas and plans	15.5%	11.8%	20.5%	13.8%	16.8%	20.6%	12.8%	12.5%
Carefully discusses and makes decisions with other leaders according to established procedure	15.5%	21.6%	6.8%	21.3%	10.5%	17.5%	15.4%	13.9%
Works to create good feelings and unity among the people	35.1%	34.3%	35.6%	25.0%	43.1%	23.8%	43.5%	40.3%

The different preferences of rural and urban parishioners lend support to the image of the rural, but not the urban, pastor as "head of the family." However, perhaps the most significant finding is the much stronger preference urban parishioners show for a leader who promotes good feelings and unity among the people. This preference is most pronounced among urban "small people" (45.5%) and least pronounced among the rural poor (16.7%). One possible explanation for this unusually wide gap is that caste, and hence caste discrimination, is a more serious problem in urban than in the more socially homogenous rural parishes. Another is that the sense of unity and good feeling in socially diverse and upwardly mobile urban parishes is in fact much more fragile and volatile, especially in the eyes of urban Dalits "in transition," than in the more stable rural parishes.

Since wise guidance and practical problem-solving are an important part of the pastor's role to so many Dalit Christians, what kinds of problems do they bring to the pastor (and other church leaders)? Personal problems of one kind or another ranked highest on the list of problems which they both do and do not discuss with their leaders. Dalit parishioners seem to keep silent about problems of which they are ashamed (personal sins and shortcomings, financial problems, family quarrels, addictions and bad habits) and share those personal difficulties which, like poverty, are part of their lives and of which they are not ashamed. Only 3.9% said that Dalit Christians "share any problem" and hide nothing of significance from their leaders.

Turning from pastors to other leaders, people saw the catechist primarily as a spiritual leader (31.2%), guide (30.1%) and to a lesser extent as problem-solver (15.6%). The role of guide, however, was especially common among rural people (42.5%), whereas the role of problem-solver was not. That particular task seems to be reserved more for the pastor! When asked an open-ended question on the subject, just over one-third of the respondents (34.7%) thought Dalit Christian women should assume new leadership roles, while the rest had more traditional views of women's roles in the church. In this men and women did not differ, but, surprisingly, both women graduates (18.1%) and women post-graduates (30.8%) suggested leadership roles less frequently than did the sample as a whole. Dalit Christian leaders received a general vote of confidence (55.5%) as champions of the Dalit Christian people, while another 14.5% said that they were the same as or better than other leaders. Especially prominent among the sceptical

26.6% minority who saw them helping only their friends and relatives were the "small people" (41%). Finally, a question was asked about the most important driving force in local church politics. A slight majority gave "the desire for personal recognition and family prestige" (50.3%) over either quarrels between individuals and families (24.8%) or competition between caste and regional groups (24.8%). These responses were spread quite evenly throughout the sample, except that very few respondents in the villages attributed it to caste and regional rivalries (11.3%), presumably because such conflicts would be less likely than the other two among socially homogenous rural Dalit Christians.

The Madras pastors responded to the questions on leadership in much the same way their parishioners did. However, a majority considered being a champion of their people's interests to be the most important characteristic of a good leader and providing clear, strong, direct guidance the most helpful form of leadership in their congregations. The Batala pastors agreed with the respondents that practical help was the most important expectation Dalit Christians had of their leaders and mentioned financial assistance as well as help with the police after drinking and fighting as the kinds of help most often needed. However, the Batala pastors considered being available was a far more important characteristic of a good leader in the eyes of their people than did either the Madras pastors or respondents. The Batala pastors also indicated that their people would consider most helpful a leader who "gives encouragement and support to the people's ideas and plans," whereas they themselves, like the Madras pastors, believed that providing clear, strong, direct guidance was even more helpful. Finally, the Batala pastors felt that their people took a dimmer view of Dalit Christian leaders than did the Madras pastors or respondents, seeing them as caught up in factional politics and thus supporting members of their own group more than the Dalit Christian people as a whole.

These findings are not in conflict with the pastors' perceptions of their roles and personal pastoral styles as presented in chapter three. Some pastors might have to modify their perceptions and style to account for a diversity and complexity greater than expected, but there are no indications here that, in ministering to Dalits, the pastors are out of touch with the reality of their pastoral situations. However, these views of leadership do provide further indirect evidence of Dalit Christian needs and inner conflicts. For example, given all the problems in their struggle for existence, it is easy to understand why so many of the rural poor would want a problem-solver for a leader. Why so many Dalit Christians see their leaders as guides is more problematic. Is it because that is the role pastors have traditionally played, and still prefer to play (as their sermons and questionnaire responses indicate), or is it because so many Dalit Christians feel genuinely confused, or even lost, in a perplexing, threatening, and changing world? Pastors to "small people' may wonder what needs lie beneath these parishioners' greater preference for leaders who can create good feelings and unity within the congregation but also their greater cynicism about Dalit Christian leaders. Perhaps they, of all Dalit Christians, are in the most insecure position and are the most frequently overlooked; perhaps they just feel that they are. Finally, the reported reluctance of Dalit Christians to share with their pastors problems of which they are ashamed would indicate that shame plays a far more powerful role in their lives than the answers to the earlier, more direct question on the subject acknowledged.

CONCLUSIONS

It is virtually impossible to summarize the findings of this chapter so as to produce a clear overall picture of how Dalit Christians see themselves, their world, their relationships, their faith, the local congregation and its leadership. The sample was very diverse and so were the responses. As a result the overall picture is one of complexity and nuance rather than of either consensus or of clear contrasts and distinctions. Perhaps this result was the inevitable consequence of relying primarily upon a superficial research instrument. Questionnaires generally reveal only what is on the surface and not what is in the inner depths of people's lives; only the public person is disclosed while the private person underneath remains hidden.[24]

---

[24] The clinician Prakash Desai's comment, "a true bipartite, two-level kind of self, may be said to reside within India. Perhaps there are multiple selves but at least there are these two selves, the public self and a private self" is relevant here. The two, he goes on to point out, are often at odds with each other. Prakash Desai, "Self-Images: Societies and Individuals under Stress," in P.C. Chatterji, ed., *Self-Images, Identity and Nationality* (Shimla, 1989), 22. I don't think India is the only place where a bipartite self resides!

Certainly the questionnaire did pick up some waves on the surface which suggest some turmoil in the depths, but even those do not allow for precise diagnosis of what is going on inside the Dalit Christian psyche. The results of the foregoing survey must therefore be treated as suggestive rather than conclusive, as an invitation to further investigation rather than as final.

It is when one looks at the clusters of responses which were unusually high or low for certain categories of Dalit Christians, instead of at the Dalit Christians as a whole, that these findings become most suggestive. Since these responses are often those of only a minority within a specific category which nonetheless contains an unusually high proportion of that particular response within the sample as a whole, these clusters represent only certain somewhat distinctive tendencies, rather than dominant views, within those categories of Dalit Christians. Moreover, not all categories show equal amounts of clustering. This survey uncovered few differences between age groups or among Dalits whose families had been Christian for differing numbers of generations. Clustering on the basis of sex or educational level was a bit more frequent, but three categories exhibit the largest number and perhaps most significant "distinctive tendencies" of all those used.

The first of these is the rural poor among whom there was more direct experience of untouchability, more fatalism, more worry and anxiety, a higher priority given to peace and contentment as the goal of life, more sense of injustice about work and income, a greater tendency to see poverty as the chief cause and psychological damage as the chief consequence of the bad treatment Dalits receive, a more communitarian outlook on being a Christian, more unity with other Dalits, and more expectation of practical help from leaders than exists among other categories of Dalit Christians. The second category is the urban middle class among whom there is less experience of untouchability, more satisfaction with work and income, more discrimination for being a Christian and less for being a Dalit (except among other Christians), more consistency in being open about one's Dalit identity, less optimism about unity with other Dalits, a more individualistic outlook on being a Christian, more desire to make the world a better place to live in, and a more widespread desire for a spiritual person as a leader than is prevalent among other categories of Dalit Christians. The third such category are the "small people" who show more signs of inner distress than do either the rural poor or the mostly urban middle class: great dissatisfaction with job and income, more perceived imitation of the high castes, more scepticism about Dalit Christian leaders, greater felt need for good feelings and unity within the congregation, and, among the women, less ability to bear shame.

It would be an oversimplification to label the rural poor as traditional, the urban middle class as modern, and perhaps the "small people" as "in transition" on the basis of these findings. In fact, any such label for what are only tendencies which are more pronounced within one category than within others would not be warranted. Nonetheless, there is some inner coherence within each of these three clusters of responses just the same. That inner coherence can provide a suggestive starting point in understanding some perhaps distinctive yet overlapping categories of Dalit Christians for the purposes of more effective ministry to them.

CHAPTER 6

PASTORAL PRIORITIES

Despite all of the diversity, complexity and ambiguity described in the preceding chapters, there are certain threads which run through their contents that need to be drawn together in order to gain some clarity of vision about ministry to Dalits. The pastor to Dalits is not a new invention; such pastors have been around for long enough to create traditions and expectations about their role. In addition, many of the challenges which they face in their pastoral situations today have been faced by their predecessors before them and are not likely to go away quickly or easily, if at all. One continuing challenge is that of sheer numbers. Whether scattered in a dozen villages or concentrated in one section of a city, there are a lot of Dalit parishioners for each pastor to care for. Although pastors do "move with the people," their ministry is carried out under the constant threat of becoming perfunctory and superficial because their contact with individual Dalits or Dalit families is of necessity fairly brief and intermittent. Consequently, what goes on beneath the surface of their Dalit parishioners' lives generally stays beneath the surface, much of it out of the pastor's sight and therefore beyond her/his capacity to minister to. What does come out instead are all the immediate practical problems the pastor is called upon to solve. This is almost to be expected because, in the rural setting, the pastors have been caught up in the role of patron, even *the* patron, for their Dalit parishioners, while their urban counterparts are "patrons in transition" to whom Dalit parishioners turn for guidance and support.[1] Practical problems take up much of the time and energy left over from the pastor's regular established responsibilities. In the eyes of many urban and rural parishioners alike, effectiveness in ministry means effectiveness in problem-solving. This has captured the pastors' attention and their vision of ministry has become focused upon the

---

[1] One gets the impression from this data that both modern equalitarian and traditional patron-client patterns of thought and behavior together shape urban pastor-parishioner relationships from both sides. Urban pastors are rarely "heads of the family," as rural pastors still are, but enough of the patron-client culture exists in the urban parishes to prevent the pastors' completing fully the transition to something else instead.

outward circumstances of their people's lives. As a result, much of what lies deeper within their Dalit parishioners' psyches appears rather blurred to their pastors and remains largely unministered to. For some pastors, changing the external circumstances of their people's lives has become the basic substance of ministry.

This chapter presents a set of priorities in seven important areas of ministry which may move pastors and congregations towards a more effective ministry to Dalits. In suggesting and discussing these priorities, the Madras and Batala pastors were guided by two important principles which are perhaps as important for ministry to Dalits as the specific priorities recommended here.

1. *Ministry to Dalits can be truly effective only if it becomes a top pastoral priority of the congregation as a whole.* If it continues to be just one among many special pastoral concerns, nothing much of significance will happen. Real ministry to Dalits will occur neither as an automatic by-product of something else nor as a result of scattered special events such as an annual Liberation Sunday celebration or outdoor healing service led by a prominent evangelist. Only if a sustained, deliberate, even somewhat single-minded and comprehensive effort is made to carry out this particular ministry may it bear some good fruit in due season. Moreover, while the pastor would be taking the lead in initiating this kind of change, ministry to Dalits is really a ministry of the entire congregation. Just as the wounds in the Dalit psyche have been inflicted by long term social relationships of inferiority, subservience, dependency and shame, so also healing and change can come through long term social relationships of respect, symmetrical reciprocity, closeness, and caring. This requires not just selected individuals but entire congregational communities to function as transforming counter-cultures within the wider society. It is based on the premise set forth by St. Paul in I Corinthians 12:26 that "if one member [of the body of Christ] suffers, all suffer together with it; if one member is honored, all rejoice together with it" (NRSV).

2. *The planning model used for bringing about change should support rather than undermine planning goals.* Perhaps the model for church planning most frequently used in India is the "problem-solution" model. Employing this model, one might review the data presented in the previous chapters of this study, decide what and where the Dalit problems are, and then prepare a set of practical steps which could be taken to "solve" those problems. However, this model has some very

serious drawbacks. The view of ministry built into it simply reinforces rather than challenges the current "problem-solver" image of ministry described above. Another disadvantage is that by focusing attention upon problems and weaknesses, it discourages, even overwhelms people, instead of motivating them to make changes. Among Dalits, however, this planning model has even more serious repercussions. It begins by awakening existing feelings of inadequacy, frustration, pessimism, and even dependency, while offering little or nothing to counteract those feelings.

The priorities described in the remainder of this chapter have therefore been developed using an "affirm and build" planning model. This planning process begins by locating and assessing not problems or weaknesses, but those things which the congregation is already good at and doing well. Then, in establishing priorities for future ministry to Dalits, one deliberately utilizes and builds upon these existing strengths. The theological assumption undergirding this model is that such strengths or strong points are God's gifts to the congregation; the congregation's planners must then decide how best to use those gifts God has already given it to better serve God's people. At the psychological level, this model conveys a positive sense of self and seems to motivate people for hope-filled change. It was built into the interview schedule used for groups of Dalit parishioners found in Appendix D. The initial brain-storming which those questions provoked was positive and at times enthusiastic. Several groups commented, with obvious delight, that they were not accustomed to think about themselves or their congregation in this way. In one parish where the translation was poor because the pastor was absent, there was total miscommunication. The questions were about strengths, and gifts, and positive assets the congregation already had; the answers were about problems, and needs, and help from outside. That experience served as a powerful reminder that the planning process one chooses carries within it the capacity to reinforce or to transform existing psychological patterns. Since transformation is a major planning goal, the planning process itself must also be transformative or the goal will probably not be realized. Moreover, when people can see and take pride in what their strengths have produced, the problems which still remain "unsolved" may not bother them so much.[2]

---

[2] Two books were especially helpful in developing this planning process: Carl S. Dudley, ed., *Building Effective Ministry: Theory and*

Of course each pastorate will have to enter into this planning process for itself, assess its existing strengths, and decide how best to build upon them so as to minister to Dalits in more effective ways. Group discussions with Dalit parishioners revealed that existing strengths worth building upon are many and varied. One village congregation had an active prayer life which had been instrumental in the healing of a neighbor who had been badly hit on the head. Another had good singing and a good women's group. Three others had considerable evangelistic zeal. One urban church considered its 140 year tradition a strength while another newer one considered "not being bound by past history" to be one of its greatest assets! Other groups of urban Dalit parishioners mentioned openness to newcomers, quality of fellowship, mission-mindedness in both social service and church planting, the location of the church building, a dynamic youth group, good singing, and a packed church every Sunday as strengths of their particular parishes. The sections which follow offer guidelines for finding ways in which strengths such as these might be developed so that the congregation as a whole might minister more effectively to Dalits.

WORSHIP

There are two important traditions to build upon in developing forms of worship which will be more meaningful to Dalits. The first is the liturgical tradition of the Indian churches. Both the Church of South India and the Church of North India have service books which contain very full liturgies not only for regular Sunday worship but also for special occasions. These are widely used in urban congregations and many members are deeply attached to them. In the villages a "freer" form of worship is generally used. The sequence usually follows a common pattern (e.g., singing, prayer, scripture reading, sermon, offering/singing, Lord's Prayer, and benediction), but the contents of each part are spontaneous and the atmosphere of worship is informal. The other tradition is the Dalit tradition of worship which the Rev. Theophilus Apavoo described to the Madras pastors as being folk-based, highly participatory, involving both music and body movement. In fact, Dalits have an unusually strong musical tradition, since providing

---

Practice in the Local Church (San Francisco, 1983); Kennon L. Callahan, *Twelve Keys to an Effective Church: Strategic Planning for Mission* (San Francisco, 1983).

music for special occasions has often been part of their customary service to jajmans.

The priorities presented here can be interpreted as incorporating more of the Dalit tradition, especially its participatory dimension, into the existing Christian tradition of worship. *Worship which is meaningful to Dalits will involve them actively and not allow them to be mere spectators; it will engage their emotions and imaginations as well as their intellects so that they worship God with their whole beings and their whole beings are affected by worship. Meaningful worship will also tap the existing strengths of the Dalit people so that they may be used for the glory of God.*

Thus, for rural worship, the pastors set greater simplicity, more shared leadership, and more music as their major priorities. Simplicity is a matter both of form ("free" worship as opposed to "prayer book" worship) and language (Dalit rather than "high" Tamil or Punjabi). Leadership can be more widely shared by calling upon members to offer prayers or give testimonies. Brief skits by members can also be used to dramatize a congregational concern or a Christian teaching so that it becomes more memorable. Sermons can engage members in discussion. Music, however, probably holds the most vital key to more meaningful worship, especially if the words give expression to what lies in the members' hearts and the tunes are folk tunes which are easily picked up and remembered. Gifted members of the congregation might be invited to compose their own songs and teach them to the congregation. The Batala pastors suggested that sermons might be built around such songs rather than scripture readings because people remember songs better. Of course, the choice of which innovations to introduce would depend upon the existing strengths of both the particular worshiping congregation and the particular pastor involved.

The two priorities lifted up for urban worship were that it become more participatory and that it include more content directly related to Dalit lives. The starting point for such innovation would be the existing service book liturgies of which many urban parishioners are quite fond. New collects and prayers can be inserted into the framework of familiar liturgies at the appropriate points. The same is also true of new songs, while brief skits could even lead into the sermon. Many urban congregations have good choirs to lead the congregation in singing new songs, and youth groups might do the skits which dramatize Dalit issues. Several pastors have found that if such innovations are first introduced on an experimental basis either on special Sundays or during evening services, they are more likely to find acceptance in the regular Sunday morning worship. In Appendix A are two examples of such liturgical adaptation and innovation. The first is an Order for Holy Communion developed as a service of healing by the Fellowship Department of Christian Medical College and Hospital in Ludhiana, Punjab. Not only does a healing service itself provide an appropriate ministry to Dalits, but it also serves as a model for adapting a very familiar liturgy in order to give it a specific focus. The second are two short prayers which might be inserted as collects within the regular liturgy. The Madras diocese of the Church of South India has prepared some Songs of New Spirituality which are available on cassette from the diocesan office. Undoubtedly others have developed similar resources as well.

PREACHING

The questionnaire survey indicated that for a majority of Dalit parishioners the sermon is the most important part of the Sunday worship service, primarily because of the teaching it offers. Judging from the sermons analyzed in chapter 4, that seems to be the way the preachers see the sermon also. However, in developing priorities for this important aspect of ministry to Dalits, the Madras pastors recommended what was referred to in chapter 4 as "strategic pastoral preaching." *Sermons should address the whole person rather than just the mind and will; they should be affirming and hope-filled rather than sin-centered and judgmental in character; and they should relate the Biblical message more directly to the present external and internal realities of Dalit life.* These priorities applied to preaching in both rural and urban congregations, but the specific changes considered necessary differed according to context.

The major innovation recommended for rural pastors was to invite discussion by the congregation during the sermon. This would draw members of the congregation more deeply into the sermon for a better appreciation of the relevance of its witness for their own lives. This may be done by posing a question and eliciting answers, by presenting a case study drawn from either the Bible or the life of the congregation for comments, by asking the congregation at the outset for their understanding of the topic or text for the day, or by asking them what they think God is trying to communicate to them through the text. The ensuing discussion, in which the pastor plays an active but not dominating or "expert" role, becomes the sermon. This type of preaching is a corporate rather than individual endeavor. (This method was not considered suitable for the towns and cities where congregations are larger in size and worship is more formal than in the villages.)

The major issue which the urban pastor faces is how to address Dalit issues meaningfully without hurting non-Dalit members and dividing the congregation. After all, the pastor has been called to serve the entire congregation and not just one section of it. The pastors considered two methods promising. One was simply to say at the outset of the sermon, or of the pertinent point within it, that what follows is addressed especially to the Dalits present; other members of the body of Christ are invited to enter into the experience of that part of the whole body as best they can and hear the good news. This method will be more acceptable to non-Dalits if used in other sermons to address the special issues of women, youth, retirees, government servants, and other categories of members because it shows that the preacher's genuine concern is to meet diverse needs within the entire congregation more directly rather than to accentuate caste divisions within the congregation. The other method is to assume a certain commonality of experience important to Dalits but shared by Dalit and non-Dalit members alike. For example, everyone in the congregation has experienced such things as anger, anxiety, self-esteem problems, identity issues, facing choices about what constitutes the good life, or seeking justice in the face of discrimination. Here the Dalit experience can be used to illumine the more general human experience in ways that are not divisive but unifying.

As this recommendation indicates, the selection and use of illustrations drawn from familiar contemporary experience play a vital role in helping both rural and urban congregation members make connections between the Biblical witness and their own lives. As indicated in chapter 4, preachers are making explicit connections with the external circumstances but not with the inner realities of Dalit Christian life. Good stories about the inner struggles of Dalits can help them, and others as well, make important connections between the Biblical witness or Christian theological affirmations and what is going on inside themselves. Parts of the pastor's own story, especially if the pastor is a Dalit, can be particularly helpful, and wise sharing of personal experience can draw pastor and congregation closer together. In sharing the experience of others, the pastor must, of course, be careful not to betray those who have shared their secrets confidentially. However, sharing at this level makes healing at this level possible; the alternative is an almost guaranteed superficiality.

PASTORAL CARE AND VISITATION

Pastoral care and visitation are the foundational work upon which ministry to Dalits is built. They are already a major priority and great strength in the total ministry of the Madras and Batala pastors. This priority is based on the premise that personal relationships are crucial in ministry to Dalits. "I know my own and my own know me" (John 10:14). *Relationships establish rapport and build trust. They also affirm personal worth and a sense of belonging, providing assurance that one is remembered and not forgotten.* These consequences of good personal relationships remain pastoral priorities of both rural and urban pastors in the three major activities of pastoral care: house visitation, counselling and guidance, and visiting the sick.

The very act of visiting is itself an affirmation of worth, remembrance and belonging. Rural pastors, accompanied by the catechist, make house visits of five to thirty minutes to each parishioner at least once a year. Appointments are not made in advance so that parishioners will not feel obligated to prepare food for the pastor. Pastors enter their parishioners' houses, even if they must bow down to do so, and accept something to eat or drink if it is offered. It is generally during such visits that pastors take the initiative in providing any personal, family, vocational, or religious counselling considered necessary, because rural Dalits will rarely come to the pastor for such help. Pastors do this by raising questions for brief discussion and then by giving advice in the light of the responses. Urban parishioners expect visits from their pastors and Dalits are apt to be offended if visited only by a lay preacher instead. Such visits are generally made in the evening around 6:30 to 8:00 PM and last from thirty minutes to an hour. In some cases appointments are made in advance. The pastor normally goes accompanied by the sexton. If urban parishioners wish counselling or guidance, they may ask for an appointment time when they can come and talk privately. Both urban and rural pastors try to make special house visits on such special days as birthdays and wedding anniversaries.

Visiting the sick is a very special form of pastoral ministry because Dalit parishioners often feel not only isolated in a hospital but guilty and depressed about their affliction as well. The rural pastor must often see that these parishioners get good medical care because the parishioners often do not know where to go for it. In visiting the sick the rural pastor will hold the patient's hand, or lay a hand upon the patient's head or shoulder, when praying and reading Bible verses which provide assurance of God's forgiveness and continuing love. The pastor must also tend to the emotional needs of the patient's relatives who are there providing what care they can. The urban pastor does much the same thing as the rural pastor when visiting the sick, but is less likely to be involved in making the initial arrangements. Consequently, it is considered especially important that the pastor visit immediately upon learning that a parishioner is seriously ill or hospitalized.

As these descriptions indicate, there are many important symbolic actions in pastoral care which communicate affirmation of worth and belonging: bowing down to enter a home, receiving food, and touching when people feel especially God-forsaken. Prayer and scripture reading also play an important role in pastoral care and visitation. The same is true of conversation. The Madras group recommended that pastoral visits be used as opportunities to encourage urban parishioners to be more open about their Dalit identity and, if necessary, to follow the example of their rural counterparts in being assertive about claiming benefits to which they as Dalits are entitled. The pastors also reported that pastoral visits were times when they had to warn rural Dalit parishioners against following those religious practices of the people around them which were contrary to Christian belief (e.g., observance of auspicious days, appeasing evil spirits and the small pox deity, or not allowing widows to participate in marriages). The Batala pastors found that personal conversations often provide the only opportunities they get to deal directly and constructively with matters of individual or collective transformation. People will listen and weigh innovations seriously when talked with personally. If these same matters are presented initially in public through sermons or at committee meetings, the immediate reaction is more apt to be counter-productive controversy coupled with strong resistance to change. These same pastors have also found personal visits to be the best opportunities available for providing basic Christian education to their parishioners.

CHRISTIAN EDUCATION

The Sunday School is generally not a great strength of either the rural or the urban congregation. Rural parishes need teachers, while in many urban parishes there are teachers but the children are more likely to be distracted by television or other activities competing for their time and attention. Adult classes are often difficult to organize and sustain. Since, as indicated in chapter 3, pastors believe that thorough teaching would be a great help to their Dalit parishioners, they rely upon other, better established means to carry out this educational ministry. Primary among these means, as is apparent in chapter 4, is the sermon itself. Other means include the after-service discussion, the pastoral visit, the women's group (which often provides the best or only adult education program in the parish), and the local Christian school which may devote an hour each week to Christian education.

What the pastors want, however, is a solid Christian education program for both children and adults which can educate in basic Christian doctrines, social issues, and Dalit liberation. They have already given priority to the development of appropriate curriculum materials, which the Madras diocese is currently preparing. In addition, rural pastors consider teacher training to be a major priority and have recommended that teachers might be selected for such training from among the better educated Christian youth.

Christian education might also be used to strengthen an already important support system for pastoral care. As indicated in chapter 5, there are certain problems which Dalit parishioners avoid discussing with their pastors. Instead these parishioners generally turn to an already existing network of family and friends for what guidance, support and help they may have to offer. Thus much of the pastor's training in counselling goes unutilized, while troubled parishioners may not get the genuine help they need. Under these circumstances, the pastor might use his training to educate interested members of the parish, who are already part of these support networks, so that they can provide more competent help when asked for it. A short series of after-service discussions in rural parishes, or special short courses at suitable times in urban parishes, could be designed not only to sensitize interested parishioners to the roots and consequences of unhealthy Dalit behavior patterns but also to show these parishioners how to help people change those patterns. In each session role playing and then discussion of fictitious but nonetheless real case studies could play a prominent part both in diagnosing problems and in finding healing ways of helping. This teaching method may help pastor and parishioners alike to discover ways to combine local "folk wisdom" with what the pastor has learned in seminary courses in order to build up the local parish as an increasingly effective caring community.

SOCIAL SERVICE AND SOCIAL ACTION

The Church in India has a long history of social service through its schools, hospitals and other institutions. In recent years it has added to these a variety of service and development programs to help the poor and needy. A priority among the Madras pastors, as well as of the Madras diocese itself, is skill development programs designed to train Dalits, including Dalit women, for jobs or self-employment. (It was the pastors' observation that Dalits are not entrepreneurs and so greatly prefer the security of a job to the risks of self-employment.)[3] Such training programs do present a positive solution to some of the poverty-related problems which Dalits bring to their pastors. It was the experience of the Batala pastors that sharing available development resources with non-Christian Dalits in the village builds solidarity. Non-Christian Dalits have been known to reciprocate by joining agitations to end religious discrimination against Christian Dalits in the award of Scheduled Caste benefits.

Social action has taken two forms. The most common so far has been the ad hoc response to a particular local crisis or incident. For example, a Batala pastor told of how his rural parishioners were being exploited by commission agents in the local market who denied them fair prices for their produce. This situation had been the source of a lot of local quarrels. The pastor therefore made his parishioners aware of how they were being exploited, and then carefully prepared them for what proved to be a successful agitation to get from the government their own license as commission agents in that market. During the Madras discussion about responding to atrocities and other local injustices, it was apparent that the relationships between local parishes and outside action groups have often been competitive rather than

---

3 This may well be more true of some Dalit groups than of others, because Dahiwale's study of Dalit entrepreneurship in Kolhapur provides contradictory evidence at this point. See *infra.*, 34.

collaborative. Activists accuse pastors and local church leaders of being mere spectators, uninterested in justice issues and doing nothing; pastors and local parish leaders see activists coming in, getting as much publicity for themselves out of the incident as possible, and then leaving the parish and its leaders to live with the continuing consequences. Obviously, some significant trust-building on both sides is necessary if this potentially invaluable form of ministry is to be more effective.

The other form of social action is the on-going work of community organization, which has become a priority for the pastors. Built into the Church of South India's VELCOM (Vision for Equipping Local Congregations for Mission) program, adopted by the Madras diocese, is a social action component which employs the problem-solution approach. It calls for an initial survey to collect data on the basis of which the parish will decide together what its most pressing needs and issues are. A trained social animator will then help the parish both to develop an action plan and to organize in order to deal with those issues and needs. Although there was no evidence in the latest diocesan report that this part of the VELCOM plan had as yet produced results which could be evaluated, the pastors remained committed to it. It may be too soon to know how effective this approach is, or it may be that only crises, rather than a deliberate planning process, can produce and sustain an effective long-term social action effort.

In both social service and social action the pastor's role has been that of go-between with outside development agencies or action groups; motivator, educator, and often organizer of local Dalits; and continuing caring presence in the midst of the pain and frustration of an on-going, day-to-day struggle.

LOCAL CHURCH GOVERNMENT

It is perhaps in local church government that the effects of social conditioning upon Dalits becomes most apparent. Dalits have been conditioned not to govern, but to be governed; to be submissive and deferential towards authority rather than to exercise authority; to seek security rather than to accept the risks of responsibility. At the same time Dalits have a strong need for recognition, status and respect which, while denied elsewhere, does find an outlet in the local congregation. It is thus not surprising that a majority of respondents saw the desire for personal recognition and family prestige as the basic dynamic of local church politics.

The behavior patterns which the pastors described in their discussion of local church government can perhaps best be interpreted as predictable outcomes of the kind of social conditioning to which Dalits have been subjected. For example, the Madras pastors described their urban Dalit parishioners as generally under-represented in pastorate committees, reluctant to serve, silent and submissive in pastorate committee meetings, and inclined to go along with the decisions of the pastor and more confident dominant groups. The Batala pastors described their Dalit parishioners as eager to hold positions of leadership but reluctant to assume the responsibilities which go with those positions. Attendance at pastorate committee meetings is often poor. The areas in which members accept responsibility are narrowly confined to trusteeship, and they leave spiritual matters to the pastor. Both sets of pastors agreed that pastorate committee elections create problems in the local parish. Of course there are exceptions, but these seem to be the general patterns.

On the face of it, there would appear to be little to affirm in this area of ministry and little therefore upon which to build. This, however, is not necessarily the case. For one thing, there is the tradition of the caste panchayat which in some areas of India was so strong that the missionaries felt that they had no alternative but to place responsibility for church government in the hands of the panchayat and its accepted leaders, if they were Christians. The Batala pastors also reported that their pastorate committees enjoy planning community functions and are very good at it. This suggests that in each parish there may be specific Dalit institutions, specific tasks, or specific individuals who provide the kind of strengths which should be affirmed and built upon.

The pastors' first priority in the area of local church government was greater participation by the Dalit members. This includes more Dalit parishioners serving in positions of respect and responsibility, their more active participation and leadership within the pastorate committees, and a broadening of the responsibilities they assume for the well-being of the pastorate. This the pastors considered an essential prerequisite for the pastors' other priority, which was giving greater importance to Dalit concerns and Dalit issues in the life of the parishes. This priority can be realized in mixed urban congregations only if Dalit members press for it and assume responsibility for it. Thus, the number and type (open, assertive, cooperative, responsible) of Dalit representatives they elect or the pastor nominates becomes very important. Some Madras pastors even suggested that the constitution be amended to assure minimal Dalit representation on pastorate committees.

In the eyes of both sets of pastors, the chief means to achieve the ends of greater Dalit participation and greater importance for Dalit concerns is leadership training for Dalit members. However, given the particular background of the Dalit members, the type of leadership training they receive is extremely important. If they are simply told what the duties of the pastorate committee are and what must be done to carry them out, Dalits may feel very ill suited for these responsibilities and so defer to others who seem to assume leadership responsibility more easily and naturally. On the other hand, if both leadership and leadership training are seen as means of transformation for those who accept it, then training can possibly change rather than simply reinforce current patterns. The existing strengths of Dalit leaders will be identified, affirmed, and developed as something of value to the entire congregation during training, so that they may find dignity and encouragement from their achievements as leaders, not just from their status as leaders. They may also need training in exercising leadership over others, not as others have exercised leadership over them, but in new, more affirming and cooperative ways. In short, the "affirm and build" model is as important in leadership development as in congregational development. In both cases the primary goal is not institutional maintenance or expansion, but human transformation in individual members as well as in the responsible and cooperative exercise of leadership.

The diocese can and has played an important role in activating, strengthening and giving a fresh mission dynamic to local church structures through leadership training and the allocation of other resources. At the same time, however, centralized decision-making tends to stifle local initiative and encourage dependency upon the benevolent wisdom of those higher up in the diocesan power structure, especially in pastorates which have little money left over after paying the diocesan assessment. This is a difficult dilemma because the diocese does not and will never have the resources to give every pastorate what it wants or needs. The Madras pastors thought that local decision-making as built into the VELCOM program's philosophy of community organization[4] as well as increased partnership between rural and urban congregations in sharing human and material resources, might be a way out of the dilemma. It could be that suitable training of second level diocesan leadership would also help this process of revitalization at the local level.

THE PASTOR'S PERSONAL LIFE

It was the pastors' considered judgment, first, that pastors to Dalits feel the impact of their ministry upon their personal lives more at three particular points than at other points and, second, that while all pastors' personal lives are affected by ministry at these three points, their impact upon the pastor to Dalits is apt to be greater. The first area of impact is the pastor's life-style. The pastor's life is an open book; pastors are expected to be truthful, disciplined, punctual, dependable, impartial, and prayerful people, free from the lures of fame, fortune, sexual promiscuity, or addiction to drink. In addition, rural pastors are expected to dress simply and eat simple food so as to remain close to their parishioners. Urban pastors, on the other hand, are expected to maintain a certain standard of living so that they are not looked down upon. This usually means that the urban pastor's spouse must have a job outside the home. In both the rural and urban cases theirs is expected to be a life-style "based on essential needs rather than on wants."

The second area of impact is time management. Since affirming the dignity and worth of Dalit parishioners is an essential part of pastoral ministry to them, Dalits take a lot of the pastor's time and attention. Dalits bring a lot of "petty things" to the pastor because they are not accustomed to dealing with those things themselves.[5] Dalit parishioners expect their pastor to be with them, available to them, visiting them. These pressures become especially acute during the wedding season. The result is that pastors have less time for their own families, for exercise, reading, Bible study, or preparing sermons, worship services and Christian education programs. Pastors' wives are

---

4 *Infra.*, 112.

5 Satish Saberwal noted a similar tendency of, or compulsion for, "the ordinary Harijan to overload the political process with relatively minor issues." *Mobile Men*, 191.

also expected to play a major role with the women of the congregation, helping them with their personal problems. Only time can tell whether or not parishioners will have similar expectations of pastors' husbands.

The third area of impact is stress. Some of the stress comes from the many demands upon the pastor's limited time and energy. Some comes from identifying with their people, sharing their oppression and shame. Some comes just from being the "head of the parish family." Occasionally politicians look to the pastors to deliver the votes of their parishioners and become vengeful if disappointed with the results. But much of the stress comes from the parishioners themselves. They bring their many wants, needs, quarrels, disputes, and anger to the pastor. Not a few question the pastor's intentions. Some circulate stories or write anonymous letters in order either to intimidate the pastor into going beyond the rules and regulations to give them what they want, or just to keep the pastor under control. In the words of one pastor, "a pastor is a Dalit hanging on a cross."

Some of the phrases the pastors used to describe how they cope were "be strong," "be in the right," "reconcile by standing for the truth," "our calling involves us in these things and so we shouldn't bother," "we have to take it easy and trust God," "we take satisfaction in doing God's work in a just cause." Underlying these phrases is a spirituality grounded in a profound sense of calling which gives inner strength, energy, resourcefulness as well as an awareness that one cannot do everything. It is a spirituality based on confidence in the grace-filled providence and mercy of God in the midst of daily turmoil. It is a spirituality which enables pastors to make choices about how to use their time and their lives in the service of their people. It is a spirituality nourished by experiences of blessing in their ministries. The pastors did not say how they cultivate this kind of spirituality, but if in the process they have found the ways through which inner healing for the self comes from God, they are in a good position to help their Dalit parishioners find similar healing.

CONCLUSIONS

Much more can and should be said about priorities in pastoral ministry to Dalit parishioners. Those stated above stay close to the findings and recommendations of the people involved in this particular study. Specialists in the various areas of ministry can perhaps expand on these priorities, pointing out their further implications or particular pitfalls, and offering possible alternatives. As has been indicated from the outset, this study is intended to be suggestive and provocative rather than definitive. Its aim has been to provide at least a temporary basis for understanding the many facets of pastoral ministry to Dalits as well as to stimulate further exploration of ministry to Dalits in greater depth and with different approaches.

What emerges from the priorities described above is a vision of a multi-faceted but focused healing ministry to Dalits. In almost every section of the chapter there is emphasis upon affirmation, participation, engaging the whole person, and opening up the inner person. The hope is that in all areas of ministry Dalits will be touched, healed and transformed by the work of the Holy Spirit at deeper levels than before. The priorities also envision the congregation, in the many aspects of its life, as a kind of counter-culture which provides opportunities for such divine healing. The pastors' role in this healing ministry is not only to use their own varied pastoral responsibilities but also to guide and coordinate the entire process of congregational transformation so that this ministry might be as effective as possible.

The centrality of such healing in the Church's total ministry to Dalits seems appropriate at this juncture in its history. This is not to suggest that the Church should set justice issues aside or that pastors should stop helping Dalit parishioners with the practical problems of their daily lives. Instead, it is simply to affirm that in and through all the works of ministry to Dalits, inner healing should now play a central role. There are at least three important reasons for giving inner healing such importance. The first and most obvious is that such healing is a good and important thing in its own right. The God to whom the Bible bears witness is a healing God who wants and works to make people whole; the healing which makes that possible needs no further justification. Another is that healing the "wounded psyche" is the Church's unique and distinctive contribution to the total Dalit struggle for dignity, equality and justice. Other agencies, organizations and action groups may well be better in promoting the struggle for justice or in assisting Dalits with their particular problems, but they do not heal. Inner healing, however, has been an essential part of the total ministry of the Church since the lifetime of Jesus himself. It should now be claimed for the Dalit struggle. Finally, it is strategically important at this historical juncture in the total Dalit struggle to give special importance to inner healing. Many might argue that priority should really be given to changing the external circumstances of Dalit lives; that true hope lies in external change because Dalits will adapt psychologically as their circumstances improve; and therefore that only when external change proves impossible should emphasis be given to psychological change itself. While there is much to be said for this point of view, it does ignore the fact that the Dalit movement itself suffers from persistent fragmentation, co-option by dominant groups, and long term ineffectiveness in part precisely because Dalit leaders remain unhealed victims of past social conditioning, seemingly unable to work with each other on an equal basis over long periods of time for the betterment of their people.[6] There are limits to what political struggle alone can accomplish for Dalits without an inner transformation taking place at the same time. This is what pastors to Dalits bring to that ongoing struggle as a unique and distinctive ministry. They begin to make that contribution by starting right where they are, as pastors, and building from there with the people God has given them to minister with.

---

[6] This analysis is supported by Lata Marugkar, *Dalit Panther Movement in Maharashtra: A Sociological Appraisal* (Bombay, 1991). This highly promising movement was not suppressed, but simply fell apart because its leaders would not, and presumably could not, work together.

APPENDIX A

LITURGICAL RESOURCES

I

AN ORDER OF HOLY COMMUNION

OPENING PRAYER & HYMN

CALL TO WORSHIP

"The Lord is my health and salvation. Truly he has borne our infirmities and healed our diseases."

Friends, we have come together to celebrate the Lord's table. Like the early church, we worship and fellowship around this table, and share in the breaking of the bread and the drinking of the cup. Christ is present with us when we gather together in his name, and in this assembly of his people we welcome him as our physician and healer.

Through the celebration of this sacrament we invoke his gift of healing and forgiveness for our work and witness. As a family and a community of God's people, we pray for the fullness of Christ in our lives. We seek God's giving and forgiving grace for us and our families, our institution, our community and country. This table gives us boldness to go out in faith, love and hope to continue the work he has commanded us to do.

(SILENCE)

FIRST READING

A CHORUS

SECOND READING

*A SHORT SERMON

HYMN

(REMEMBRANCE/SPECIAL OCCASIONS)

CONFESSION:

O God, our health and salvation, we bring before thee the brokenness, the ill-health and the disease in and around us. We confess before thee that there is no health in us. Our relationships are broken. We have sinned against thee and against one another. We come to thee seeking your forgiveness and pardon for us. Restore us to the fullness of Christ and the joy of salvation, according to your promise in Christ Jesus, our Lord and Master. This we ask in his name. Amen.

INTERCESSION:

Leader: Lord, we pray for the world you love so much and for which you gave your only begotten son, Jesus Christ. We pray for people ravaged by war, hunger, disease and injustice. We bring before thee communities living in fear, insecurity, ignorance or ill-health.

We remember before thee families torn by suspicion, distrust, anxiety, suffering or pain.

We pray for those who are in distress, sickness, loneliness or in sorrow.

Response: Lord send thy healing and health upon us and thy world.

Leader: We pray for our country, its leaders and those in authority. We remember the churches in our country, their people and leaders.

We pray for the healing ministry of the Indian Church, particularly for Christian Medical College & Hospital, Ludhiana. And finally we pray for ourselves and for our families.

Response: Lord, hear our prayer.

Leader and People: We commend ourselves to thy unfailing love and mercy, and commit ourselves to thy unfinished task before us. We ask of thee thy infinite resources to carry out the mandate you have given to us and thy Church. Give us the unction of the Holy Spirit which leads us into all truth, that thy purposes and plans may be fulfilled in and through us. Amen.

ANNOUNCEMENTS

OFFERTORY HYMN (Elements are brought forward)

OFFERTORY PRAYER (All)

Be present, be present, O Jesus, the good and high priest, as thou wast in the midst of thy disciples, and make thyself known to us in the breaking of the bread, who livest and reignest with the Father and the Holy Spirit, world without end. Amen.

THE COMMUNION

Minister: Lord Jesus, you command us to celebrate this table till you come again. You made us partners together in the work of reconciliation and salvation of the world. You made us your friends and agents of your healing in a broken and wounded world. This bread and this cup are symbols of your goodness and love towards us. Quicken us by your life, empower us with your love and inspire us by your Spirit. As we take part in this feast of thanksgiving and praise, help us to be living and witnessing members of the body of Christ. Build us as a community of faith, enable us to accept one another as Christ accepted us, forgiving one another as Christ forgave us. Equip us to fulfill the love of Christ in a wounded world, hurt and hurting.

"In the same night that he was betrayed, he took bread and after giving you thanks, he broke it, gave it to his disciples, and said, 'Take, eat, this is my body which is given for you. Do this in remembrance of me.' Again, after supper he took the cup and having given you thanks, he gave it to them and said, 'Drink this, all of you, for this is my blood of the new covenant, which is shed for you and for many, for the forgiveness of sins. Do this, as often as you drink it, in remembrance of me.'"

People: Christ has died.

Christ is risen.

Christ shall come again.

Minister: This Eucharist/Holy Communion is our daily bread, given at the table of sacrifice, the altar of suffering. It is here, with Jesus, we can offer our own pain, and the pain of the world, to the Father. The broken bread, the broken body of Jesus, draws us towards the rejected, the hurt and the poor. In them, and through them too, our hearts are fed, often in a painful way. Let us also share in the pain of our crucified Savior and Lord.

Together: We do not presume to come to this your table, merciful Lord, trusting in our own righteousness, but in your manifold and great mercies. We are not worthy so much as to gather up the crumbs under your table. But you are the same Lord whose nature is always to have mercy. Grant us, therefore, gracious Lord, so to eat the flesh of your dear son, Jesus Christ, and to drink his blood, that our sinful bodies and

souls may be made clean by his most precious body and blood, and that
we may evermore dwell in him and he in us. Amen.

Minister: Draw near in faith. Receive this holy sacrament with
faith and thanksgiving. Whenever we eat this bread and drink this cup
we proclaim the Lord's death until he comes again.

(People receive communion. A song is gently sung)

PRAYER OF THANKSGIVING

Almighty God, we thank you for feeding us from your table. As
living members of your Church, send us into the world outside, to love
and serve you, to tend the wounds of our world, to comfort and heal all
who are in pain or sorrow. This we ask for Christ's sake. Amen.

BLESSING

May the blessing of God the Father, who is our refuge and hope,
Jesus Christ our Saviour and Lord into whose healing ministry we have
been called, and the Holy Spirit who guides and leads us into all truth,
rest and abide with us, now and for ever. Amen.

*CLOSING HYMN

CLOSING PRAYER (Ex Tempore)

AT THE DOOR:

Minister: Go forth into the wide world, be witnesses to the saving
and healing power of Christ.

People: Amen.

* Optional

(*Ministry of Healing.* Fellowship Department, Christian Medical
College and Hospital, Ludhiana, Punjab. Courtesy of Chaplain Jaiwant
Noel.)

II

TWO BRIEF PRAYERS

A Prayer Based upon the Lord's Prayer

Our God, who is near to and far away from us, glorified be your name in our everyday living. Your plans be executed in all our struggles as they were carried out in the exodus-event. Help us satisfy this day all our needs. Forgive us our being passive and indifferent members of this unjust social order. Allow us not into bondage of any sort, but set us free from the state of being oppressed and exploited. For yours is the universe, all our lives, struggles and services. Amen.

(Paul S. Elisa)

A Prayer Based upon Portions of Psalms 69, 55, & 3.

O God, for it is for thy sake that we have borne reproach, that shame has covered our face. We have become strangers to our upper caste Christians. It is not an enemy who taunts us -- then we could bear it. It was not an adversary who deals insolently with us -- then we could hide from them. But it is our companions, our familiar friends. We used to hold sweet converse together; within God's house we walked in fellowship. Many are saying of us, "there is no help for them in God." But thou, O Lord, art a shield about us, our glory and the lifter of our head. Amen.

(V. Devasahayam)

APPENDIX B

PARISH INFORMATION FORM

GENERAL

1. Your name   **Are you a Dalit?**

2. Year of birth   **Year of Ordination**

3. Name & location of the parish/pastorate

4. Is your parish/pastorate urban or rural?

5. How many parishes are in your pastorate?

6. Of these parishes how many have Dalit members?

7. How many years have you been pastor there?

8. Are you the only pastor there or do other pastors serve with you?

9. Are there catechists serving there with you?   How many?

STATISTICS

If you are serving a pastorate with more than one parish in it, please pick one parish and answer <u>all</u> the remaining questions in this section and the next <u>with reference to that one parish only</u>. If your pastorate has only one parish, then answer with reference to that parish.

It is extremely important to be as accurate as possible in answering the questions in this section because the answers you give may provide the basis for later statistical calculations.

10. How many Christian families are there is this parish of yours?

11. Of these Christian families, how many are Dalits?

12. How many non-Christian Dalit families would you estimate live within the boundaries of this parish?

13. What percentage of the Dalit Christians in this parish are:
    a. illiterate? ___%
    b. have a primary education? ___%
    c. have a matric or secondary education? ___%
    d. are graduates or postgraduates? ___%
    TOTAL 100%

14. What three occupations give employment to the largest percentage of the Dalit Christians in this parish?
    a. ___%
    b. ___%
    c. ___%

15. What percentage of the Dalit Christians in this parish would you describe as:
    a. Poor, or without steady income ___%
    b. Working class ___%
    c. Middle Class/professional ___%
    d. Educated but without steady employment ___%
    e. Other (specify) ___%
    TOTAL 100%

PASTORAL

16. In this parish what three activities <u>actually</u> take up most of your time and energy?
    a.
    b.
    c.

17. What three activities take up most of the catechist's time and energy?
    a.
    b.
    c.

18. In this parish what three activities do you <u>wish</u> took up most of
    your time and energy?

    a.

    b.

    c.

19. In this parish what do you consider to be the three most serious
    needs of the Dalit Christians?

    a.

    b

    c.

20. Are these needs different from the needs of the other Christians in
    this parish?

21. Are these needs different from those of non-Christian Dalits in that
    area?

22. What do you consider to be the two greatest difficulties in being a
    pastor to Dalits?

    a.

    b.

23. What have been the 2 most serious obstacles in the way of Dalit
    Christians in this parish becoming what God intends them to be?

    a.

    b.

24. Can you name 2 or 3 important ways in which the Church as a
    whole and you as pastor have been able to help the Dalit Christians
    in this parish become more truly what God intends them to be?

    a.

    b.

    c.

25. Can you name 2 or 3 important ways in which the Church as a
    whole and you as pastor have been unable to help Dalit Christians
    in this parish become more truly what God intends them to be?

    a.

b.

c.

Thank you very much for filling out this questionnaire. Please bring the completed questionnaire along with copies of your most recent Christmas sermon, your most recent Easter sermon, and one other of your best sermons to the opening session of the consultation.

INTERVIEW SCHEDULE FOR PASTORS

1. Are you experiencing difficulties in administering the questionnaire?

2. Clarify any ambiguities in their parish information form.

3. Get some personal background
   Family
   Education
   Decision to enter ministry
   Seminary
   Previous pastorates
   Assignment here:
     How and why made?
     How do you feel about it?
     How does your family feel about it?
   Hopes and plans for the future

4. What are your responsibilities in this pastorate or parish?

5. What do you consider this parish's greatest strengths to be?

6. What do you think your own greatest strengths as a pastor are?

7. How would you describe your own leadership style? (Possible references to questions 72 & 75)

8. So then, how do you work with this congregation?

9. What would you consider the major results to have been so far?

10. On the basis of this and your previous experience, what ways of pastoring Dalits have you found most effective?

11. Is either alcoholism or domestic abuse more common among Dalits than among other Christians in this parish?

INTERVIEW SCHEDULE FOR PARISH GROUPS

1. Personal introductions

2. Please tell me some of the history of this church.

3. What do you consider some of this church's present strengths to be?

4. What do you think this church does best?

5. What do you think the greatest strengths of your pastor are?

6. What do you think he does best?

7. Now, if you were to develop and use these strengths which God has given to this church even more than you already have, what do you think might happen in and through this church?

8. If you had an opportunity to tell a group of pastors what you as a lay person consider to be the best (most effective) ways of pastoring Dalits, what would you say to them?

9. In your experience, is it more common and more acceptable for Dalit Christians to reveal their Dalit background now than previously?

QUESTIONNAIRE

Note: In this questionnaire there are two types of questions. In one, there are a limited number of possible answers given to the respondent and the respondent chooses the most appropriate one. The others are open-ended questions to which individual responses were listed. Later, after reading through all the responses to the question, categories were developed to place them in. Those categories are printed here in italics to distinguish them from the multiple-choice responses to the first type of question. In each case, the numbers in parentheses are the total number of people who gave the response indicated next to the number.

PERSONAL

1. Name (optional)_____

2. Pastorate/parish: a. rural (80)
                 b. urban middle class (70)
                 c. urban poor/working class (25)

3. Sex: a. male (102)   b. female (73)

4. Age: a. under 30   (42)
        b. 30-45   (57)
        c. 46-60   (52)
        d. over 60   (24)

5. Education:
  a. None   (10)
  b. Primary School   (17)
  c. Middle School   (30)
  d. Matric   (58)
  e. BA/BSc.   (26)
  f. MA/MSc.   (27)
  g. Other (specify) _____ (6)

6. Occupation
   a. *housewife*   (7)
   b. *unskilled daily wage labor*   (27)
   c. *farmer, small business or craft (rural)*   (14)
   d. *skilled labor*   (15)
   e. *teacher*   (27)
   f. *office worker*   (18)
   g. *professional/officer in government or business*   (16)
   h. *rural church worker*   (10)
   i. *retired*   (22)
   j. *student/unemployed*   (14)
   k. *other* _____   (4)

7. Married?   a. yes (145)   b. no (30)

8. Spouse' occupation
   a. *housewife*   (21)
   b. *unskilled daily wage labor*   (20)
   c. *farmer, small business or craft (rural)*   (6)
   d. *skilled labor*   (11)
   e. *teacher*   (21)
   f. *office worker*   (3)
   g. *professional/officer in government or business*   (15)
   h. *rural church worker*   (1)
   i. *retired*   (10)
   j. *student/unemployed*   (3)
   k. *other* _____   (9)

9. Subcaste _____

10. In your opinion, within the Christian community, you are among
    the:
    a. elaikal (poor)   (63)
    b. siriya vanika (small people)   (39)
    c. natuttara makkal (middle class)   (72)
    d. periya vanaka (big people)   (1)

11. Are you?
    a. first generation Christian   (43)

b. second generation Christian (50)
c. third generation Christian   (62)
d. fourth generation Christian   (15)
e. more than fourth generation Christian (5)

OUTLOOK

12. Which of these statements comes closest to your own views?
    a. Being rich or poor is a matter of your destiny; you cannot do anything (23)
    b. I can improve my circumstances and those of my family (151)

13. Which of these statements comes closest to your own views?
    a. The world is evil and life is the story of pain and suffering (44)
    b. The world is a good place and life is a wonderful gift (129)

14. Which of these statements comes closest to your own views?
    a. The present conditions of our society cannot be changed (28)
    b. The present conditions of our society can be changed (147)

15. Which of these statements comes closest to your own views?
    a. Health, happiness, disease, misfortune are all due to chance (50)
    b. No, these are the consequences primarily of human actions (124)

16. Which of these statements comes closest to your own views?
    a. My position in life today is due to my fate or my karma (11)
    b. My position in life today is due to my own achievements (125)
    c. My position in life today is due to the influence of society (10)
    d. My position in life today is due to the help of certain people (29)

17. Which of these statements comes closest to your own views?
    a. My grandchildren will be better off in every way than I am (150)
    b. My grandchildren will be about the same as I am (18)
    c. My grandchildren will be worse off than I am (3)

18. Which of these statements best expresses the purpose of your life?
    a. To be content and at peace (90)
    b. To make the world a better place for myself and for others (55)
    c. To do my duty (21)

d. To be successful (8)
e. Can't say (1)

DISPOSITION

19. Which of these phrases best describes you these days?
    a. A person who is content (133)
    b. A person who is worried, anxious, or frustrated (42)

20. Which of these phrases best describes you these days?
    a. I am a person with many weaknesses (64)
    b. I am a person with many strengths (110)

21. Which of these phrases best describes you these days?
    a. I am a person who can tolerate any situation of shame (128)
    b. I am a person who cannot bear shame (47)

22. Which of these phrases best describes you these days?
    a. I am prepared to risk conflict in order to help change things (129)
    b. I prefer peace and harmony and so to let things be as they are (46)

23. Would you say that you feel angry
    a. all the time (0)
    b. most of the time (11)
    c. some of the time (156)
    d. almost never (7)

24. What is the surest way to get you angry?
    a. *Insult to my dignity or pride* (54)
    b. *Frustration / disappointment* (32)
    c. *Being lied to or cheated* (27)
    d. *Opposition* (21)
    e. *Injustice* (27)
    f. *Other* (13)

25. When you do feel angry, what do you generally do?
    a. *Lash out verbally* (78)
    b. *Lash out physically* (10)
    c. *Turn it inward* (56)

d. Escape (14)
e. Pray (13)

26. All people have fear. What is your fear?
    a. Fear of God's rejection (76)
    b. Fear of spouse / in-laws (8)
    c. Fear of devil / demons/ Satan/ darkness (12)
    d. Fear of future events I cannot control (42)
    e. Fear of my own weaknesses / mistakes (27)
    f. Nothing (6)
    g. Other _____ (3)

27. When you pray, what do you pray for most frequently?
    a. Family well-being (79)
    b. Health (14)
    c. Basic needs (10)
    d. Peace / joy / salvation (21)
    e. The Church and its ministry (13)
    f. Other people (31)
    g. Other ___ (6)

28. When your mind wanders, what do you think about most often?
    a. Myself; my problems, hopes and worries (51)
    b. My family (74)
    c. Helping others (14)
    d. Social problems (14)
    e. Life with God (16)
    f. Other (5)

IDENTITY

29. When you describe yourself to other people, which of these labels do you generally use?
    a. Harijan (7)
    b. Dalit (9)
    c. Christian (116)
    d. Protestant (13)
    e. Church of South India (7)
    f. Scheduled Caste (15)

g. By jati (0)
h. By occupation or job title (9)
i. Other _____ (1)

30. Which do you prefer to be called?
    a. Christian (111)
    b. Dalit Christian (62)

31. Which of these statements comes closest to your own views?
    a. I am proud to be a Dalit (135)
    b. I am ashamed to be a Dalit (21)
    c. I am cursed to be a Dalit (10)

32. Which of these statements comes closest to your own views?
    a. Dalit Christians must be cautious in affirming their Dalit origins openly (61)
    b. Dalit Christians must take the risk of affirming their origins openly in order to experience their freedom (61)
    c. It is a requirement of faithful Christian living to affirm one's Dalit origins openly (47)

33. Do you disclose your caste identity?
    a. never (15)
    b. only among close friends or members of my caste (30)
    c. only on matters related to the government's reservation policy **(14)**
    d. only when asked (77)
    e. on all occasions (39)

34. Why do you consider yourself a Christian? (rank importance 1,2,3,only)
    a. I was born in a Christian family (61)
    b. I belong to the Christian community (13)
    c. I was baptized (19)
    d. I follow the teachings of Jesus (26)
    e. I have faith in God and in Jesus (54)
    f. I attend church services regularly (2)
    g. I give money to the church (0)
    h. I receive the Lord's Supper (0)
    i. Other _____ (0)

j. I don't know (2)

35. Why do you remain a Christian?
    a. To be a witness (82)
    b. For my own salvation (23)
    c. To worship the true God (34)
    d. Christ's teachings are the best (14)
    e. To serve others in Christ's way (15)
    f. Other _____ (7)

RELATIONSHIPS

36. Is untouchability still being practiced where you live and work?
    a. Yes (68)
    b. No (107)

37. If yes, give one or two of the most common examples of it.
    a. Does not apply (88)
    b. Denied housing or entry into homes/shops (22)
    c. Food exchanges refused (14)
    d. Subservient behavior demanded (10)
    e. Physical proximity avoided (16)
    f. Other (7)

38. Where untouchability is practiced, is any distinction made between Christian and non-Christian Dalits?
    a. Does not apply (46)
    b. Yes (60)
    c. No (62)

39. Do you feel that your caste is still a barrier to your advancement?
    a. Yes (43)
    b. No (81)
    c. No, but being a Christian is a barrier (50)

40. Are there social groups and social occasions from which you are excluded because you are a Dalit?
    a. Yes (66)
    b. No (88)

c. No, but I am sometimes excluded because I am a Christian (21)

41. Do Christians where you live and work practice untouchability?
    a. Yes (32)
    b. No (123)
    c. No, but they discriminate against us in other ways (19)

42. Please give one or two of the most common examples.
    a. *Subservient behavior is demanded* (1)
    b. *No real fellowship is offered* (32)
    c. *They go to separate churches* (5)
    d. *They don't want intermarriage with us* (6)
    e. *Does not apply* (92)

43. What do you think is the main reason why other castes treat Dalits so badly?
    a. Because we are poor (59)
    b. Because we do menial work (6)
    c. Because we are less educated (20)
    d. As punishment for our sins (0)
    e. Because their religion says we are unclean (1)
    f. Because of caste prejudice (67)
    g. Because it is in their economic interests to do so (7)
    h. Because they wish to control us (12)
    i. Other (specify) _____ (1)

44. In my opinion the worst consequences of the caste system have been
    a. *Social divisions and alienation* (38)
    b. *Social inequality, discrimination, and oppression* (44)
    c. *Bonded labor / slavery* (12)
    d. *Degradation, psychological damage* (46)
    e. *Communal violence* (32)

45. Have you availed yourself of any of the facilities offered by the government to the Scheduled Castes/Backward Classes?
    a. No (122)
    b. Scholarships (35)
    c. Job (5)

d. Development assistance (12)
e. Other (specify) _____ (2)

46. Do you think that your present job and income are in accordance
    with your merits?
    a. Yes (95)
    b. No (79)

47. Where you live and work are relationships between Christian and
    non-Christian Dalits
    a. Excellent (13)
    b. Good (78)
    c. Satisfactory (70)
    d. Poor (11)
    e. Very bad (2)

48. On what issues should the Christian and non-Christian Dalits join
    hands together?
    a. For political reasons (40)
    b. For basic safety and security of life (38)
    c. To get our basic needs met (31)
    d. For respect and dignity (29)
    e. To make social and economic progress (35)

49. Do you think this will happen?
    a. Yes (159)
    b. No (15)

50. Why?
    a. Because it is already happening and proving successful (22)
    b. We share a common plight (32)
    c. It is in our interests to do so (16)
    d. It is our best hope for a good life (41)
    e. We are already neighbors (20)
    f. Unity is strength (21)

51. Some Dalit Christians, upon getting education and jobs, think they
    have become big people; others are always ready to help their

fellow Dalit Christians. In your experience do such Dalit Christians help other Dalit Christians?
a. Usually (12)
b. About half the time (46)
c. Occasionally (88)
d. Never (24)

52. Which statement comes closest to your own views?
a. The welfare of the Dalits lies in their harmony with the high castes (76)
b. The high castes will always misuse the Dalits (96)

53. Is it important for you to have fellowship with other Dalit Christians?
a. Very important (72)
b. Important (96)
c. not important (6)
d. harmful (1)

54. In order to improve their status Dalit Christians imitate the food habits and dowry system of the higher castes.
a. Agree (75)
b. Disagree (98)

55. Among most Dalit Christians in this congregation, who controls the family income?
a. Husband (54)
b. Wife (24)
c. Husband controls his income; wife controls hers (8)
d. Both share control of the combined income (85)

56. What difference do you see between Dalit Christian women and other Dalit women?
a. Education (32)
b. Hygiene (5)
c. Better habits and life style (65)
d. Psychologically different (21)
e. Better religious life (18)
f. Not much difference (32)

57. The contrast between Christian and non-Christian Dalit women is greater than the contrast between Christian and non-Christian men.
   a. Yes (109)
   b. No (66)

BASIC BELIEFS

58. In practice which of these are the two most important sources for your understanding of what you should believe and do as a Christian?
   a. Tradition (18)
   b. Other people (2)
   c. Parents (69)
   d. Bible (78)
   e. Sunday worship (9)
   f. The pastor (0)
   g. Other Church leaders (1)
   h. Other Christian books (1)
   i. Other (specify) (0)
   j. Don't know (0)

59. The Bible describes salvation in many different ways. Which of these understandings of salvation have you personally found most meaningful?
   a. Going to heaven (41)
   b. Forgiveness of my sins (63)
   c. Liberation of the oppressed (37)
   d. Abundant life for believers here and now (27)
   e. New heaven and a new earth (7)

60. How does Jesus Christ help you in your everyday life?
   a. *Guidance* (43)
   b. *Support* (39)
   c. *Companionship* (29)
   d. *Problem-solver* (23)
   e. *Bestower of benefits* (39)

61.What kinds of gifts does Christ give to Dalit Christians?
   a. *Material benefits* (26)

b. Spiritual gifts (54)
c. A new quality of life (37)
d. Ability to deal with life's challenges (28)
e. A calling / vocation (6)
f. The Church (5)
g. Salvation (7)
h. No special gifts (7)

62. Does Christ give those same gifts to other Dalits?
    a. Yes (133)
    b. No (37)

63. Was Jesus a Dalit?
    a. Yes (98)
    b. No (41)
    c. Not sure (35)

THE CHURCH

64. Why do you go to church services?
    a. Custom/habit (2)
    b. Because other Christians do (0)
    c. To be with my friends (1)
    d. It is my Christian duty (16)
    e. To worship God (102)
    f. To seek God's favor (25)
    g. To learn more about my faith (23)
    h. To gain spiritual satisfaction (7)
    i. To get clarification of my doctrinal doubts and questions (1)
    j. Other (specify) _____ (0)
    k. Don't know (0)

65. Which part of the service is the most important to you?
    a. Singing (26)
    b. Prayers (31)
    c. Sermon (92)
    d. Lord's Supper (16)
    e. Other (specify) (2)

66. Why?
    a. (Answers to this question were not tabulated.)

67. How does worship help you with your daily life?
    a. It doesn't (4)
    b. Don't know (14)
    c. *It provides fellowship and community* (19)
    d. *It provides guidance in leading a Christian life* (57)
    e. *I receive spiritual and psychological benefit* (76)

68. What do you think God wants this congregation to do in the next 3 years?
    a. Don't know (14)
    b. Remain as it is (13)
    c. *Building construction work* (37)
    d. *Evangelism / church growth* (44)
    e. *Improve quality of spiritual life* (15)
    f. *Be of greater service to others, especially the poor* (23)
    g. *Greater fellowship and unity in the church* (19)

69. Everyone has a favorite wish for their church. What is your number one wish for this congregation?
    a. *Become a model congregation* (10)
    b. *Growth through evangelism* (46)
    c. *Growth in quality of spiritual life and Christian unity* (59)
    d. *Improved social service and social justice ministry* (25)
    e. *Improvement in physical plant* (27)

70. Which of these statements comes closest to your own views
    a. I like Sunday worship the way it is (84)
    b. Sunday worship must change to include more participation of members (89)

LEADERSHIP

71. People expect many different things from their leaders. What do you think are the most important things Dalit Christians in this congregation expect of their leaders?
    a. *A good Christian Character* (42)

b. A person who treats people with love, care, patience, fairness (48)
c. A person who helps us with our problems in practical ways (69)
d. A person who is active in seeing that justice is done (14)

72. Which of these do you think is the most important characteristic of a good Church leader?
   a. Must be a spiritual person (41)
   b. Must be available to the church members when needed (2)
   c. Must be a wise and clear teacher and guide (82)
   d. Must be a courageous champion of the people's interests (43)
   e. Must have good political connections in Church and government (8)

73. What kinds of problems do the Dalit Christians here bring to the pastor or other Church leaders?
   a. Church problems (29)
   b. Personal problems (96)
   c. Quarrels and disputes (26)
   d. Problems in the lives of other people (15)

74. What kinds of problems do the Dalit Christians here avoid bringing to the pastor or other Church leaders?
   a. Personal sins and shortcomings (95)
   b. Personal financial problems (19)
   c. Property disputes (5)
   d. Addictions (20)
   e. Fights with other members (7)
   f. They share any problem (6)
   g. No response (11)

75. Which kind of leader do you think would be most helpful in this congregation?
   a. A leader who gives clear, strong, direct guidance to the people (58)
   b. A leader who gives encouragement and support to the people's ideas and plans (27)
   c. A leader who carefully discusses a makes decisions with other leaders according to established procedure (27)
   d. A leader who works to create good feelings and unity among the people (61)

e. Don't know (1)

76. How do people see the catechist?
   a. Spiritual leader (54)
   b. Administrator (13)
   c. Problem-solver (27)
   d. Friend (11)
   e. Guide (52)
   f. Does not apply (16)

77. What new roles in the Church do you think Dalit Christian women should play?
   a. *Leadership roles* (58)
   b. *Service roles* (38)
   c. *Spiritual roles* (42)
   d. *No new roles* (19)

78. Which of these statements comes closest to your own views?
   a. The most important driving force in the politics of the local church is a desire for personal recognition and family prestige (83)
   b. The most important driving force in the politics of the local church is the quarrels between individuals and families (41)
   c. The most important driving force in the politics of the local church is competition between caste or regional groups (41)

79. Which of these statements comes closest to your own views?
   a. Dalit Christian leaders are the same as other leaders, if not better (25)
   b. Dalit Christian leaders are proud and arrogant and do not serve the people (6)
   c. Dalit Christian leaders help only their relatives and friends (46)
   d. Dalit Christian leaders are champions of the Dalit Christian people (96)

APPENDIX F

LIST OF PARTICIPANTS

MADRAS

Rev. Augustine Andrews, St. Thomas Garrison Church, Madras
Rev. D.E.S. Arulchandran, Tamil Evangelical Lutheran Church, Purasawalkam, Madras
Rev. E.W. Christopher, Wesley Church, Royapettah, Madras
Rev. Y.L. Babu Rao, Redeemer Church, Madras
Rev. Rajan Devakumar, Madavaram-Pannur Pastorate
Rev. B. Devaprasad, Periyapalayam Pastorate
Rev. Paul S. Elisa, Arcot Kuppam Pastorate
Rev. Samuel Jacob, St. Michael's Church, Padi, Madras
Rev. Lawrence Jebadoss, Arakkonam South Pastorate
Rev. A. Karunakaran, CSI House of Prayer, Adyar, Madras
Rev. Stanley Kirubakaran, Sriperumbadur Pastorate
Rev. Gunasekaran Koilpillai, Melrosapuram Pastorate, Guduvancherry
Rev. Bramwell Samuel Kumar, Ennore Pastorate, Madras
Rev. Stephen Michael, Arakkonam North Pastorate
Rev. Martin J. Philip, Uthukottai Pastorate
Rev. Francis Rajadoss, St. Thomas English Church, Madras
Rev. Jacob Selvan, Nemili Pastorate
Rev. S. Sigamoni, Nagari Pastorate
Rev. Ida Swamidoss, St. Barnabas Church, Madras

BATALA

Rev. Ajeet Kumar, Christ Church, Kasauli, H.P.
Rev. Ram Lal, CNI Church, Pathankot, Punjab
Rev. Sohan Lal, Naldera, H.P.
Rev. Sunil A. Luke, Epiphany Church, Amritsar, Punjab
Rev. Mustaq A. Malk, St. Mary's Church, Kotgarh, H.P.
Rev. Edwin Ram, St. Thomas Church, Tarn Taran, Punjab

APPENDIX G

GLOSSARY

Adi Dravida: first or original Dravidians
Basti: urban neighborhood
Bhangi: sweeper jati in North India
Biradari: caste brotherhood
Biri: rolled-leaf cigarette
Chaudhari: hereditary headman
Cheri: a separate hamlet inhabited by Dalits on the edge of the village
Dalit: broken or oppressed; the label increasingly preferred by those
    previously called untouchables, outcastes, or scheduled castes
Darbar: royal court
Goonda: a lawless person
Jajman: patron
Jajmani: hereditary patron-client relationship
Jati: an endogamous caste unit
Kam karnewala: worker, client in a jajmani relationship
Lambardar: headman of a village or part of a village
Mai-bap: mother-father
Mohalla: urban neighborhood
Padre: pastor
Panchayat: a council of five members
Puja: an act of worship
Pujari: a priest responsible for temple worship
Zamindar: landlord